HEAVY

As I read Todd's book, it was as if it were my own journey. One of the most difficult things in the journey is watching your wife and family react. One of the advantages of this book is that Todd's wife contributes from her journal, so you get not only the patient perspective but the primary caregiver.

—*Ed Dobson, Author/PALS (Person with ALS)*

If you find yourself in the midst of suffering, you know that the weightiest words of encouragement and hope come from those who have suffered as well. Todd and Kristin have experienced pain on the deepest level, and they offer a candid account of where they see God in the midst of it.

—*JJ Heller, Singer/Songwriter*

HEAVY

FINDING MEANING AFTER A TERMINAL DIAGNOSIS
A Young Family's First Year with ALS

Kristin Neva and Todd Neva

THE
CHRISTMAS TREE
HOUSE

Published by The Christmas Tree House
Hancock, MI 49930 U.S.A.

ISBN 978-0615917580

To our children, Sara and Isaac

May you know and love the God
who gives rest to those who carry heavy burdens.

We love you.

CONTENTS

INTRODUCTION

"We read to know we are not alone," the character, C. S. Lewis, said in the movie *Shadowlands*.[1] In June of 2010, Todd was diagnosed with ALS. Amyotrophic lateral sclerosis, also known as Lou Gehrig's disease, is a progressive muscular-neurological disease that results in total paralysis and eventual death, usually in three to five years. In our grief, we were comforted by books written by others who face grief and disability.

In addition to reading, we wrote of our thoughts, feelings, and experiences during the year after the diagnosis. Kristin wrote in her journal and we both wrote on the CaringBridge website.

Our writings have found their way onto the pages of this book. Many other books tackle the topic of facing a terminal disease retrospectively, often from the spouse's perspective, or from the patient after some time has passed. *Heavy*, instead, follows the gut-wrenching first year after the diagnosis. Our story is told from Todd's perspective with journal entries by Kristin at the end of each chapter.

We read that, when facing ALS, it often takes a year for some sense of (new) normalcy to return.[2] We couldn't write this book today; it could only have been written when the emotions were raw. And it is our hope that our story will help you—in your suffering, in your grief—to know you are not alone.

PROLOGUE

My four-year-old daughter, Sara, and I stood in the glow of the bonfire on the east shore of Swan Lake. At home, on the lake, the stars are bigger and there are more of them. I was on vacation at my parents' home, where I grew up, in Northern Minnesota, to go deer hunting in early November. My wife, Kristin, Sara, and Isaac, my one-year-old son, came along to visit my parents.

"This is a magical place," I told Sara.

"Why is it magical? Are there fairies here? Do they sprinkle fairy dust?"

"This is the most special place on earth—right here. This is where I developed my superhero powers."

Sara knew me as a superhero dad, but she did not understand that I had a big chunk of kryptonite in my pocket.

This far north, one always finds the Big Dipper, even if it is low in the sky. On occasion, the Aurora Borealis visits. After roasting marshmallows, we backed away from the fire and lay on our backs. "Do you see the glow?" I asked Sara, pointing above us with my right arm, still strong enough to hold above my head. "That's the Milky Way." I wanted Sara to experience my childhood.

I woke at 5:45 the next morning. Deer hunting was to begin a half hour before sunrise. From a hunting blind—a tent with zippered windows on each side—set on the west side of a field, I watched Venus rise, then the sun. I sat there for four days, morning and evening, alone. In my normal routine, I can barely sit still for a minute, but there I was hunting—silent and still— perhaps one last time before I become mute and motionless. As I sat, I thought back to the prior year when the world started getting heavy.

1.

BEING BLINDSIDED

Even though I walk through the valley of the shadow of death, I will fear no evil for you are with me; your rod and your staff, they comfort me.
—*Psalm 23:4*

My life began when I was three, or maybe four, playing cowboy. I had *bona fide* boots and a belt. That was my first memory. I wish I could remember earlier events, but I can't. The first memories of my disease are vague like that. My new life began November, or maybe October, 2009, when I unstrapped Sara from her car seat.

"Come on, let's go," I said as I tried to lift her out of the van. My right arm worked, but my left didn't. *This is strange. Let's try this again. She is all of thirty-two pounds. It shouldn't be that hard.* I grabbed Sara from underneath her arms and tried to lift her again. Sure enough, my right arm worked and my left didn't. I managed to get her out by tipping her to the side, primarily using my right arm.

Over the Christmas holiday, I discussed with Kristin's family how my left arm didn't seem to work. To illustrate, I grabbed a three-pound jogging weight. Trying to curl it, I said, "It feels like twenty-five pounds." I thought maybe it was a pinched nerve, so I made an appointment with a chiropractor for the following week.

"Have you been in an accident?" my chiropractor asked, pointing at the x-ray showing my neck curved forward, instead of backward.

"No."

He measured the force of my grip. My right hand scored ninety-five pounds, but my left hand scored only fifteen. After a few adjustments, I got relief, and since my neck curved the wrong way, I thought I had found the source of the weakness. I continued to see the chiropractor for a few months. My left hand grip strength improved to forty pounds, but strangely my right hand deteriorated to ninety, then to eighty-five.

I didn't think about my arm much except for when strange episodes occurred. One day in March, walking from my office to a conference room, I grabbed coffee and a muffin from the cafeteria. I balanced the muffin on top of my notebook, using it like a tray, holding it with my left hand. I held the cup of coffee with my right. As if a concrete block had been placed on my notebook, my left arm gave out. I braced the notebook against the wall with my body, unable to move without dropping the muffin or spilling the coffee. I stood in that position for about ten seconds until the plant fire chief came up from behind me and asked, "Do you need a hand?"

"Can you carry my muffin and coffee to the conference room?" I asked, conscious of the strange request. I would have to make such requests more frequently in the coming months.

My arm was getting worse, so I stepped up my efforts to find relief. I tried massage, I found another chiropractor, and I looked into physical therapy.

After months of seeing the chiropractor and with my arm still getting weaker, my primary care doctor referred me to a spine care clinic for physical therapy.

At the spine care clinic, I gave the neurologist the x-ray showing my neck curved forward. He felt my neck and looked at my left arm. The doctor said my symptoms had advanced too far, with noticeable atrophy on my left side. He canceled my physical therapy, which had been scheduled immediately following the exam, and said that I should have an MRI as soon as possible. He said I would need to be open to neck surgery. I got the MRI a few days later, then Kristin and I returned the next week for a follow-up appointment.

At the follow-up appointment, rather than immediately discussing the MRI results, the doctor proceeded to give me a more thorough clinical examination. He pushed and pulled on my arms and legs, had me walk on my heels and toes, gently touched with a tissue my fingers and toes, shined a light across my skin, and checked my reflexes.

Then the doctor pulled up the MRI and said my neck was fine.

"Oh," I said, "that's a relief."

"It may be something far worse. It could be ALS, but I'm not sure. I want you to see a neurologist who specializes in ALS," he said.

I wasn't shocked, stunned, or in denial. I simply did not believe the doctor's suggestion that I might have ALS. Kristin reacted calmly, so I figured she, like me, assumed the doctor was speculating on a worst-case scenario that would turn out to be nothing—a benign neuropathy. On the drive home, our conversation turned to daily life.

In the meantime, I thought to myself, *This is nothing like what Danny had.* Danny, a family friend, had died a year earlier from ALS. It came on so suddenly the doctors first thought he had a stroke. The progression of the disease was fast—he became paralyzed, and then, in a hospital bed in his home, he died a year and a half after his diagnosis. That was my understanding of ALS. *I do not have it*, I convinced myself.

We had a busy evening getting the kids fed and put to bed. I started cleaning the kitchen while Kristin lay upstairs next to Isaac until he fell asleep. Forty minutes later, I was still cleaning the kitchen when I heard loud weeping from the living room. I rushed in to find Kristin on the computer. On the screen was information about ALS. Amyotrophic lateral sclerosis, also known as Lou Gehrig's disease, destroys the connections between the brain and voluntary muscles, leaving its victims paralyzed, even unable to swallow and breathe. The average life expectancy is three to five years from diagnosis; some live longer, but with limited mobility. All this happens while cognitive functions remain intact.

There is no known cause, no cure, and no treatment.

"He's wrong." I held her and said, "I'm fine, this is just a big mistake and everything is going to be okay."

For the next couple weeks, until I saw an ALS specialist, we researched the disease. We also researched other possible causes of weakness. We were not yet convinced I had ALS. As we approached the appointment on June 11, I told Kristin I would go alone to see the specialist. "The doctor will confirm this is not ALS, and then I'll be off to see other specialists."

"Don't you want me there for moral support?" she asked, although it would mean she'd have to find childcare for our children, Sara and Isaac.

"No, I'll be fine."

The nurse weighed me—212 pounds in my cowboy boots—then led me to Exam Room 1. She took my vitals—low blood pressure and a slow pulse, even for a big guy. "Put this on." She handed me a gown. I looked at the garment with three arm-openings. "Your arms go in here and here," the nurse said, sensing my confusion, "then wrap it around again and put your right arm in here." She left the room.

Wrapped in the thin gown, I sat on the edge of the examination table waiting for the doctor. He arrived a few minutes later, introduced himself, then got right to the point. "The doctor thinks you have ALS?" the specialist asked.

"He just wanted you to take a look at me. I don't think it's ALS, because I only have weakness in one arm," I said, sure of my research.

"When did you first notice weakness?"

"I put in a patio a year ago May. The bricks were heavy, but they were bricks. I don't think I had a problem then. I had trouble picking up my daughter last fall, perhaps October or November."

"Your symptoms started last May?"

"No, last fall," I clarified.

He began his examination. He pushed and pulled on my arms and legs and wrote down numbers. He had me walk on my heels and toes. He took a flashlight and put his face close to my legs and watched… for several seconds. He did the same to my back and to my arms. He pricked me with pins, tickled me with tissue, and checked my reflexes by hitting a spot underneath the kneecap that made my leg jump.

The specialist excused himself from the room and asked me to change back into my clothes. Returning a few minutes later, he positioned a chair across from me and said in a calm voice, "Well, I think the doctor was correct. This looks like ALS."

Like an accident victim blacking out details of the crash, I don't remember what I said next. I must have pressed for details.

"You have signs of both upper and lower motor neuron death. You have atrophy, weakness, fasciculations (muscle twitching), hyperreflexia, muscle spasticity, and cramping."

"But I only have weakness in my left arm."

"You have weakness in your right hand, too. People swear up and down they were perfectly strong a week prior, but I can tell they've had months or years of motor-neuron damage. You are a typical case of single limb onset," the ALS specialist explained. "At this point it is still only possible, given the four levels of diagnosis being possible, probable, likely, and certain."

After letting the words sink in, I asked, "Is this really a diagnosis? Because I need to get more life insurance." *I have to take care of my family. I have to protect them.*

"That's probably not an option," he replied.

My heart sank. I looked at him in stunned disbelief. *I can't tell Kristin. There's no need for her to worry.*

It was June 11, 2010. My new life had begun.

For a few minutes, I thought I could protect Kristin by keeping it from her until I found another cause, but I realized protection should not come from isolation. Kristin and I tell each other everything. Early in our relationship, I withdrew from conflict, but she dragged it out of me every time. We communicate even when it is hard. That openness in our relationship has built a trust cemented in stone.

The rest of the day was a blur after the specialist spoke those fateful words. I cannot remember if I called Kristin on the drive home or if I waited to tell her in person, but I told her.

That night, as we lay in bed and I held Kristin, we cried and we prayed. We prayed, "Oh, God, please let this be a mistake. Please let this be anything else."

Before drifting to sleep, I said, "Kristin, he said 'possible ALS.' We still do not know for sure this is ALS."

Our church sanctuary is my place of surrender. It is the place where I lay my burdens before God. I am stoic at work and strong at home, but, at church, I humble myself before God. Although God is with us everywhere, the sanctuary is where I come to worship Him.

On the Sunday following my diagnosis, we went to church like any normal Sunday. We had cried pretty much all the way from Friday through Saturday night. In the rush to get the kids ready and out the door, we were too distracted to dwell on our grief.

As we entered the sanctuary, I had a difficult time holding back my emotions. We found a pew toward the rear of the sanctuary. When the music started, the congregation rose and began to sing *Here I Am to Worship*, a song from our wedding. The floodgates opened. I ran out of the sanctuary, through the lobby passing Toby, the assistant pastor and our small group leader. I ran down the steps, through the parking lot, and into the field beside the church. Toby followed close behind. I fell to my knees, sobbing, and cried out, "Oh, God! Oh, God!"

Toby knelt beside me and put his hand on my shoulder. "Todd, are you okay? What's wrong, man?"

"The doctors think I have ALS. I think they're right. I can tell something is wrong with my body. I can feel fireworks going off inside," I said, regaining my composure, "muscles twitching throughout my body."

Toby prayed for me, and then he asked, "Can I share this with others for prayer?"

"Of course, I need prayer more than I need privacy."

I couldn't go back into the church. I knew I would lose it again. When I had convinced Toby I was okay, he went back in. I walked around the church. When I came around the back, I saw Kristin, who had been walking around the other side to find me. I started to weep again. Kristin cried, too. We walked toward each other and embraced.

KRISTIN'S JOURNAL, JUNE 2010:
How Will We Cope?

In the days after Todd's diagnosis, I was in shock. I couldn't sleep. I functioned on adrenaline to take care of Sara and Isaac. My mind raced with many thoughts: "Jesus, why don't You come back now? Put an end to all this pain and suffering. Let's have life the way it was intended to be."

In the past, when I thought about Christ returning, I hoped it would be later—after I got married, after I had kids, after my kids got married and had kids. Well, now I pray for Him to come back today. I do not want to face life alone without Todd; we are a team, and I want my children to have their daddy.

I was comforted a little when someone told me that this isn't fair, but kids are resilient and Sara and Isaac will be okay. I hope that is true. Still, as a mom, it kills me that it will be normal for my children to not have their daddy.

There is so much pain in this world; I am only now more aware. A youth pastor I had worked with in Chicago lost his wife to cancer. I found his blog about their journey and her death. She died at age thirty-seven after a four-year battle. They had two little boys. I cried as I read their story.

"It is so unfair," I told Todd. "They were following God. Good marriage. Happy family."

"So you think it would be more fair if only drug dealers got sick?" Todd asked.

"Yup. If only there were a correlation: You have ALS; you must have been dealing drugs. You have cancer; you must have been stealing."

Todd says then we would come to God for the wrong reasons, just for the blessings and not for Him.

I read the blog looking for answers because their situation seemed as bad as ours. How did they cope? How did the boys cope? They lived with family after his wife died. He had his boys sleeping on the floor in his bedroom. They adjusted, and that gives me hope that somehow we will too.

OUR PRAYER

God, this is a huge shock. The carpet has been pulled out from under our feet. We fall flat on the hard floor, and it hurts. God, we believe You are there, solid beneath us.

2 SAMUEL 22:3 *God is my rock,*
in whom I take refuge.

2.

GRIEVING WELL

Blessed are those who mourn,
for they will be comforted.
—*Matthew 5:4*

I struggle with understanding the sovereignty of God: Although He hasn't healed me, He seemed to protect me and my family in other ways in the week after the diagnosis.

For one thing, the diagnosis came when most of my family was vacationing together and could comfort each other. My brother's daughter had just graduated from high school, so my parents and sisters were with his family on the Atlantic coast. My mother was an emotional wreck, and it ruined the family vacation, but it was good that she was with family. It was her dear friend who lost her son, Danny, to ALS. It ravaged his body. He lost functionality so fast he could not adapt, always one step behind. That is what my mother knew of ALS.

Also, weeks before, Kristin's parents had planned to visit the weekend of June 11. After my diagnosis, we were not fully functioning, but they arrived that evening to take care of the kids and to comfort us.

I did my best to convince Kristin all was okay, which calmed her a bit, but she was not entirely buying it. I was not as confident as I sounded. I kept it together pretty well, except one morning when I got out of bed early after lying awake most of the night feeling the twitching all over my body like fireworks. I had this dreaded sense that my body was not okay—that the doctor was right. At 5:30 a.m., I went downstairs so as not to disturb Kristin's sleep. Kristin's mother, Lani, was awake too, or at least she was sleeping lightly and awoke when she heard me approach her room. I began to cry, and I told her, "I think they're right. Something is wrong with me. I think this really is ALS."

Lani wept, and then prayed, words sputtering out between cries.

I wondered, in hindsight, if God's hand was in that—making sure my parents had the support of my siblings, and making sure we had the support of Kristin's parents. But if His hand was in that, why doesn't He go all the way and heal my body from this disease?

We found hope after my diagnosis in the word "possible." I reminded Kristin, "The ALS specialist said it was 'possible ALS,' not 'probable,' not 'certain.'" We read an article saying misdiagnoses occur ten percent of the time. "It is a mistake. It has to be a mistake. Nothing unusual or rare ever happens to me."

I waffled between deep sadness that I had a terminal disease and being mad the doctor had come to such a quick conclusion, especially when there were so many other possible causes of my symptoms. I've had twitching for years, cramping for decades, and my hyperreflexia goes back to childhood—I once kicked a doctor when he tested my reflexes, not hard, but enough to elicit a chuckle.

There are tests one wants to pass, and tests one wants to fail. One week after the initial diagnosis, I went in for a nerve conduction test and an electromyogram (EMG) to confirm the diagnosis. A diagnosis of ALS is a process of elimination; the doctor first needed to rule out all other possible causes of the weakness. In the nerve conduction test, a technician placed electrodes on my body and ran a current—an electric shock—to see how fast the signal moved up and down my arm and leg. The results showed my nerves responding well, and I said, "Great," as if I'd gotten results back that my cholesterol was low. Kristin, who had done research on the tests, said that we were actually hoping the test would have shown a problem. Passing the nerve conduction test confirmed that I did not have a neuropathy—non-fatal peripheral nerve damage.

The next phase of the test involved the ALS specialist sticking needles into my muscles. As I activated each muscle, he listened to the static representing the neuromuscular signals. Quiet was good. Static was bad. I didn't have any benchmark to which to compare myself, but I could tell that some muscles were louder than others.

After the EMG, we waited in the cold, uncomfortable examination room. Kristin sat on a stool, and I sat on a hard plastic chair. The neurologist returned. "I am afraid my suspicions were correct." He upgraded the diagnosis from possible to probable ALS.

"How can we know for sure?" I asked.

"If the disease continues to progress, it becomes more certain."

I hadn't had many experiences with deep, personal grief. I once grieved the loss of a job when I was a young man, twenty-three years old. Soon after, I suffered the rejection of a girlfriend.

I knew in my head that I would be better by far without the job and the girl, but my heart still took years to heal. I grieved the loss of a pregnancy, of an unborn child, as Kristin's doctor was "100% sure" that she had an ectopic pregnancy, that the baby was in a fallopian tube. Kristin went in for lathroscopic surgery. The grief was short-lived, as the doctor, to her surprise, found that Kristin had a healthy pregnancy and Sara was born seven months later.

I lost uncles and aunts, grandfathers and grandmothers, and a step-grandmother. I held my mother when she grieved the loss of my elderly great aunt, with whom she lived for a few years. I sat by my father as he wiped tears from his eyes with his hand-kerchief at his mother's funeral—she died at age ninety-four. I've not known what to say when comforting others in grief, but I knew that there is a process people must go through and they must do it well. Grief, like love, should be an action, not just a feeling. I routinely signed sympathy cards with the words, "Grieve Well." But my unlearned advice, to grieve well, hardly prepared me for the feelings that came with being told that I had a terminal disease with a three- to five-year life expectancy.

The pain I feel is not just from what I am losing. The pain is for others in my life who will be affected by my death.

Kristin is too young to be a widow. She will lose the help of her partner. She will have to carry most of the load of caring for the kids while she becomes my full-time caregiver. Then she will lose me, her husband who loves her unconditionally.

It pains me to think that my one-year-old son may not even remember me and the life lessons I have yet to teach him. I have yet to teach him how to be a man, how to ride a bike, and how to treat a woman. I have yet to attend his ballgames. My boy needs his dad.

My heart aches that my four-year-old daughter will not have her dad to teach her when to have the oil changed in her car. I want to model how a man ought to treat her. I have yet to walk her down the aisle at her wedding. My girl needs her dad.

I hate the thought that parents may attend their own child's funeral. In comforting my mother, I told her not to count me out: "I still plan to attend your funeral."

She responded, "Then, I'm going to live to 100."

KRISTIN'S JOURNAL, JUNE 2010:
Why Doesn't God Take Away the Pain?

I heard a blood curdling scream that I knew came from my little boy. I ran to the bathroom and I saw his fingers flattened in the hinged side of the closed door. Sara had shut the door as Isaac was trying to follow her into the bathroom.

I screamed, opened the door, and scooped him up. Seeing my little boy in pain hurt my heart and I tried my best to make him feel better. He wailed as I ran to the sink and held his hand under cold running water. Isaac calmed down enough for me to breastfeed him, and then he started crying again. I measured out liquid pain reliever and squirted it into his mouth in between sobs. Then I cuddled Isaac and sang to him as he fell asleep with his head against my shoulder. I rocked him for a while longer, and then put him in his crib. When he woke, he was okay. His fingers were bruised and blistered, but he was happy and playing again.

The book of Matthew says, "If you, then, though you are evil, know how to give good gifts to your children, how much more will your Father in heaven give good gifts to those who ask him!" (7:11) As a mom, I don't like to see my children hurting. I step in. I comfort them. I protect them. I do everything in my power to soothe them. Doesn't God feel the same way? Then why doesn't He heal Todd? Why doesn't He take away our pain?

I can understand how some pain in this world might be beneficial. It makes us long for Heaven. But what good could there be in my children losing their father?

Todd says God doesn't promise healing, but He gives love, joy and peace.

OUR PRAYER

God, we don't understand why this is happening. Comfort us, Lord. Give us Your love, joy, and peace.

2 CORINTHIANS 1:5 *For just as the sufferings of Christ flow over into our lives, so also through Christ our comfort overflows.*

3.

ENJOYING
THE MOMENT

This is the day the Lord has made;
let us rejoice and be glad in it.
—*Psalm 118:24*

The sweetest things are not those with the most sugar, but the desserts that come after dieting. That was the sweetness of Father's Day, two days after my diagnosis was upgraded from "possible" to "probable" ALS. There were no grand plans for the day. Kristin and I had too much on our minds.

"What would you like to do today for Father's Day?" Kristin asked as we ate breakfast on Sunday morning.

"I don't know."

"How about going to the zoo?"

"Yea, the zoo!" Sara decided for us. Sara was oblivious to all that was going on.

First we went to church. I still had difficulty sitting through the worship, but I managed to hold back my tears. After the service, a friend approached gingerly and asked how I was doing. I started to cry, and then quickly regained my composure. I told him, "I am okay." He backed away. Some guys are full of advice, while others don't know what to say; they all care in their own way.

We made our way out of church, stopping several times as people offered their sympathy and support. As Kristin and I strapped the kids into the van, she asked me, "What do you want to do for lunch?"

"Let's pick up food and bring it home."

When we arrived home, Kristin unstrapped Sara from her car seat and Sara dashed off to the yellow disc swing hanging from the branch of the Norway pine in the front yard.

"It's a beautiful day, let's eat outside," I said. Kristin agreed, and I placed Isaac on the lawn and then pulled the picnic blanket out of the back of the van. Isaac was ten months old, and he was on the move. I had to retrieve him twice and put him back in the middle of the lawn before I could get the blanket spread out.

Kristin called for Sara to come join us. We settled down on the lawn with the doors of the van open so we could hear the JJ Heller CD. Sara sang along, "When my world is shaking, heaven stands. When my heart is breaking, I never leave your hands."[3] The song had come to have deeper meaning to me and Kristin, but Sara just loved the music and she had all the words memorized.

Kristin went into the house and retrieved two cards that she and Sara made. In my card from Kristin, she wrote, "You are a good husband and a good father." Sara wrote, "DAD - LOVE - SARA," and she drew a picture of us. *She is a budding artist. I am so proud of her.*

We cleaned up after our picnic and headed over to the zoo, where fathers were admitted free on that day. It's a small zoo, but it has lions and tigers and bears, nonetheless, and monkeys and giraffes too. And it's beautiful, built on a bluff overlooking Lake Michigan.

We pushed Isaac around and he pointed at the animals. Sara leaned in close to Isaac and told him, "Look, Isaac, that's a penguin." *I'm glad they have each other.*

We took a train ride around the zoo—a miniature train, not on tracks, with a little engine that pulled half a dozen cars along a walking path. After the train ride, we sat on a park bench and snacked on oranges while we overlooked the lake. Sara ran down the hill, met new friends, and picked dandelions.

Having a terminal diagnosis makes me so appreciative of the time that I have with my family. On that day, there was no grand plan, no fancy Hallmark card, no neat gadget for a present. It was a simple, sweet day with my family—the gift of time—and my best Father's Day ever.

KRISTIN'S JOURNAL, JUNE 2010: *What's the Purpose?*

"God, we pray that this is not ALS, but if it is, we pray that the suffering will not be wasted," our pastor prayed for us the Sunday after Todd's diagnosis. I pondered his prayer. I know suffering is part of life. Even Jesus suffered, but as Jesus went to the cross, praying, "not my will but yours be done," He knew the purpose of the suffering He was about to face; it was part of God's purpose to save us when we put our faith in Him.

I wish I knew what the purpose is in Todd having ALS. It seems so senseless. I do not want this life, especially for my kids. I want to wake up and find out that this was a bad dream. I want my happy life back. Instead, I am trying to figure out how to live well. I don't want Sara and Isaac to grow up in a depressed, angry atmosphere. We don't know what is going to happen in life; so much of it is out of our control.

After church, we stopped at the store. As we got out of the van and put Isaac in his stroller, it started to sprinkle. Pushing Isaac in the stroller, Todd ran into the store while I walked behind under the umbrella holding Sara's hand. She was being a typical, pokey four-year-old. The wind picked up and it was difficult to walk as it pressed against the umbrella. I picked up Sara and tried to run with her, but our umbrella blew inside out and I couldn't move. I stood there, struggling, and was about to let go of the umbrella when a man ran out of the store and grabbed it for me. We dashed into the store, which was dark due to a power outage, and joined Todd and Isaac. We watched the rain pound against the windows. I had never seen such a strong wind.

We found out later a tornado had touched down less than a mile from where we stood in the parking lot. It was a good reminder, in light of what we are facing, that life can be over in a blink. The only choice we have in our situation is to try to live as well as we can and trust that God has a greater purpose in this even if we don't like it and can't see it. By the time we left the store, the storm was over and the sun was shining. I hope the sun will come out in our lives, too.

OUR PRAYER

God, life is so fragile. It can be over in a blink. Help us remember that life on this earth is temporary. Thank You for the time that we have. Let us use that time well.

PSALM 90:12 *Teach us to number our days aright, that we may gain a heart of wisdom.*

4.

LIVING
IN THE NOW

Therefore do not worry about tomorrow,
for tomorrow will worry about itself. Each
day has enough trouble of its own.
—*Matthew 6:34*

We'd make a great team," I told Connie, my blind masseuse. "You lost your sight; I will lose everything except my sight." Over the Fourth of July weekend, we visited Kristin's parents in the Upper Peninsula of Michigan, and they treated Kristin and me to massages with Connie. They have known her for years. My father-in-law goes to her for back massages; his well drilling business is hard on his body. So Connie knew of my then-recent diagnosis. Everybody who suffers a significant loss has a unique journey. My journey is not the same as Connie's, but I could relate to her struggles.

"How are you doing?" she asked as she began the massage. She was not asking about my health; I had already explained my symptoms and what I needed her to work on. Rather, she was asking about my state of mind with informed empathy—credibility in her voice—because she has also dealt with great personal loss.

"I am okay," I said, unconvincingly. Connie worked my arm muscles like pulling paste out of a large tube of toothpaste—squeezing my forearm, and then pulling down to my wrist. I wasn't ready to explain how I was feeling; I could barely understand it myself, so I turned the conversation: "How did you lose your sight?"

"I was nineteen years old and attending college to become a nurse. Because of my diabetes, I was having problems with my eyes. They tried an experimental laser treatment on me, but it created scarring. I woke one day and couldn't see except for out of my peripheral vision, but I went to class, anyhow, with my head turned to the side. My professor sent me home." Connie's vision came back that day, but then later that evening when she was in her bedroom, everything went black. She screamed and her dad came running. It is that moment when everything has changed that bonds all who suffer a significant loss.

Massaging my muscles, Connie told me her story. I cried, glad that she could not see my tears. Twenty-some years ago, Connie suffered the loss of her dreams. She tried to continue school, but needed to drop out due to the obvious impracticality of being a blind nurse. Her boyfriend, whom she had hoped to marry, couldn't handle her disability and broke up with her. I thought about the dreams that I was losing—advancing my career, growing old with my wife, and watching my kids become fine adults.

Connie was frustrated with her new limitations, but she eventually found purpose and meaning as she adapted to a new world, experienced only by touch, taste, sound, and smell. She became a massage therapist and her world opened up through her physical interaction with people. *Will I be able to adapt to total paralysis? Will I find meaning when I am a motionless mass?*

Connie learned to live with a disability, and more importantly, she learned to live without thinking of her disability.

Could I do the same? I thought about ALS constantly as I lifted things to observe how heavy they were and observed my muscles to see if there was any atrophy. I was driving myself nuts. It reminded me of a decade earlier. After having LASIK surgery, my eyes were not perfectly balanced. Observing a clock across the room, using only my left eye, my vision was clear, but with only my right eye, my vision was blurry. The doctor told me that my eyes were fine—20/10 and 20/20—only slightly different, and that I was going to drive myself nuts by obsessing over it. I took his advice and tried as hard as I could to keep both eyes open all the time, or both closed, as it were. It worked; I stopped thinking about my vision. Maybe that would work for some disabilities. But there will come a time when my disability will become so debilitating that I cannot imagine not thinking about it. I will need to learn to deal with it when the time comes. But, until then, I mustn't allow the disability to be salient in my thoughts. I mustn't let my thoughts ruin these better days.

At times, Connie lived with a cloud over her head because of all the possible complications from Type I diabetes. She was worried and stressed, but then decided that if she was going to live, she couldn't worry about the future. She told her doctor, "You have to stop telling me all the things that can go wrong, or I won't see you anymore." I'm not particularly interested in knowing the future challenges I will face with ALS, either. I know I will eventually have trouble swallowing, and will likely get a feeding tube. I will have trouble breathing and will need to decide if I should get a ventilator, but I'm not there yet, so I'd rather not even think about it.

At first, Connie was angry at God, but she eventually found comfort in Jesus Christ. She encouraged me to live one day at a time—to live in the now. I was grieving, and that was fine. Grief is healthy and should not be rushed. But as important as the grief was, I needed to live without a sense of dread and worry.

Living in the now does not mean living recklessly or without consideration for the future; there are still things that we need a plan for, such as finances. Living in the now means that I shouldn't obsess on my current health and all that could go wrong. I need to focus on what I have today and enjoy it. I will face challenges in the future, and I will have to make tough choices, but I will cross those bridges when I come to them.

KRISTIN'S JOURNAL, JULY 2010:
New Perspective

When we visited my parents over the Fourth of July weekend, my dad took all of us—my mom, Todd, the kids and me—out on Portage Lake in his small fishing boat. There are only three seats in the boat, so we brought along a couple lawn chairs. As I put life jackets on the kids, Todd set up a lawn chair for me to sit on. He pushed it down, and it sprung out and hit my big toe. My toe throbbed and blood seeped out from under my toenail. Todd apologized. "I'm okay." I said. I sat in the boat, trying to enjoy our boat ride, thinking, "Limited time. Enjoy each moment. I wish my toe would quit throbbing so I could."

My toe felt much better the next day, and we went to a park to let the kids play. As we stood by the van, I helped Todd as he tried to get Isaac's shorts on with his one good arm. As we wrestled our squirmy toddler, Todd accidentally stepped on my sore toe, again apologizing.

That evening, Todd grabbed my foot affectionately. "Watch the toe." I laughed, amused to find that my main reaction to Todd repeatedly battering my toe was one of gratitude. I was thankful he was there to make my toe bleed.

Todd's diagnosis has changed the dynamics in our marriage. In the past, I have addressed conflict head-on: when we had a difference of opinion in parenting, when I thought one of his jokes was crude, when I perceived him as being bossy.

On occasion, I get annoyed and go in the bathroom and close the door. "I'm thankful he is here to irritate me," I vent and I let it go. Does it really matter? It's not that important. I'm just glad he is still here.

OUR PRAYER
God, help us to live in the now, with love and grace for each other.

PROVERBS *12:16 A fool shows his annoyance at once, but a prudent man overlooks an insult.*

5.

THINKING OF TOMORROW

In his heart a man plans his course,
but the Lord determines his steps.
—*Proverbs 16:9*

Jesus spoke the words "do not worry about tomorrow," knowing the future that was ahead of Him. Even as the hour of His death drew near, He, a true leader building a legacy, prepared His apostles. I, too, must be a leader for my family. The weekend after the diagnosis, I purchased three journals, one each for Kristin, Sara, and Isaac.

I wrote to Kristin about how much I loved her. When we were dating, I bought her flowers that included a generic note, "To: Kristin, From: Todd." She politely thanked me. The next time I bought her flowers, I had the florist write, "To: My NT From: Your NF," alluding to the Myers-Briggs personality inventory that we were studying at the time. (Kristin's character type is NT, Intuitive Thinking, while my type is NF, Intuitive Feeling.[4]) Kristin went on and on about the note, and I realized that the flowers were an expensive envelope. During our first year of marriage, I wrote her a letter every month on the date of our wedding. I had slacked off significantly over eight years of marriage, but was writing to her again.

In the journals to the kids, I first wrote that I was proud of them and that I loved them very much. Years ago, I heard a sermon titled "A Cup Running Over." The pastor talked about God's love being so plentiful in our lives that we would be free to share it. In raising his kids, the pastor attempted to make them feel so loved and so secure that they would show Christ's love to other people.[5] I pray that I'll be around for a long time so that my kids will know the extent of my love for them, personally, but these journals are my legacy—things that will outlast me, things that they can keep close to their hearts—so the kids can keep their cups running over.

The best laid plans often go awry. I was frustrated, realizing a new limitation, when my hand would cramp after writing short entries. The rest of the journals would need to be electronic.

While not worrying about the future, I needed to think of the financial security for my family. As I previously mentioned, my first reaction after receiving my diagnosis was to ask if it would prevent me from getting more life insurance. More insurance was not an option, but I at least have a modest life insurance benefit and long-term disability through my company.

The best I could tell, Kristin and the kids would be okay, at least financially, which significantly improved my outlook on the whole situation. Although I was a finance manager with an MBA, I wanted reassurance that we had a solid financial plan. We got a referral for a Certified Financial Planner, a friend of a friend and fellow Christian who agreed to advise us *pro bono*. He drew up a plan, which was not dissimilar to mine. Kristin has somebody to consult when I am no longer around to advise her. A burden was lifted from my shoulders.

Planning for my family's emotional and financial needs was not enough. I also had to think of their physical needs and the practical support helpful for raising a young family.

I have a sense that I will not progress as fast as Danny had, but that will make mobility all the more important as I may be in a wheelchair for a longer time. Our beautiful 1925 bungalow is not handicap-accessible. There are steps to get into the house, narrow doorways, and a hallway that turns ninety degrees to access the bedrooms and a small bathroom on the main floor. The basement and two bedrooms upstairs would be entirely inaccessible, once the motor neurons in my legs die. And the view out the living room is of a cemetery—not what I want to see while I'm dying.

I've asked myself if it would be better to go fast or to go slow. Not that I can choose, but I'd rather go slow, and be a presence in my children's lives. I want to get out of the house and attend their musical and athletic events. While in the house I want to look out windows at a beautiful view. Most important, I want my family to have the support of Kristin's parents nearby.

"We need to sell the house," I told Kristin. "We need to build next to your parents. Danny required a lot of care, so I know you cannot do it alone. We have good friends in Racine, but friends are not family." We need to sell the house and move to the Upper Peninsula. Kristin is from the U.P. and her parents live on the property where Kristin was raised. My vision is to build a house on that land so that Kristin would have her parents' support as she becomes my full-time caregiver.

I started designing my dream house. The house was grand: 2,500 square feet with a vaulted ceiling and large windows overlooking the field. It had a great room concept with a loft hanging over the kitchen and dining area where we could put a whole bunch of throw pillows and the kids could play video games. That was the dream, not constrained by the reality of how much it would cost to build. I would learn to dream smaller.

Once we decided to sell, there was a lot of work in getting the house ready, including finishing a half-renovated room. My brother drove over from Michigan at the beginning of July 2010 to help me scrape windows and paint walls.

I was frustrated working on the room with a weak left arm. I used to love renovation work. I always had a project going, and, over a six-year period, we spent thousands of dollars renovating our home. I didn't think of those projects as investments. The work was my hobby and I enjoyed it, but I didn't like renovation work anymore. My left hand couldn't hold a screw in place while my right hand turned the screwdriver. I couldn't hold a tray of joint compound as my right arm worked the mud into cracks of the plaster. My last big house project did not feel like the projects that had come before—it was drudgery. But with my brother's help, I finished the room. It was beautiful.

We listed the house with a real-estate agent in July 2010.

Planning for the future helped me worry less about tomorrow, although worrying less about tomorrow didn't negate the grief.

KRISTIN'S JOURNAL, JULY 2010:
Making Memories

I look at life with more appreciation than I did before Todd's diagnosis. Yesterday, I sat in my peaceful backyard on the brick patio that Todd laid, surrounded by the beauty of the flowers and tomatoes that Sara and I planted. The feel of sunshine on my face and the sound of insects brought joy. I watched Sara and Isaac play in the sandbox, thankful that we have two children. Last night, Todd told me, "I love you so much, Kristin," and I knew he meant it, even more than before.

I am thankful for the memories we are making. Today, on my birthday, I woke up to flowers, a card, and a book. Then, Todd took us all to the outlet mall to buy me a new Coach purse. "I want to buy you a pink purse," Sara declared with excitement. After we picked out my new purse—I convinced Sara we should go with black—we sat on a bench in the sun and watched people walk by while we ate kettle corn and drank lemonade. The day is a beautiful memory I will always have of our family together.

Squeezing in memories is bittersweet. Last weekend, we took Sara and Isaac to the beach. The sun sparkled off the water as Isaac pointed at the seagulls flying over Lake Michigan. I took pictures as Todd went into the water with the kids; Isaac splashed near the shore and Sara dunked up to her neck. We don't have as many pictures of Isaac with his daddy, so I took a lot of the two of them. As I snapped away, I was aware that I was taking pictures for the future. Someday, I would be telling Isaac, "See how Daddy was strong enough to pick you up." I would show him the picture of Todd kissing him on his head. "Daddy loved you, Isaac."

I am thankful for the time we have, but it is a painful kind of gratitude.

OUR PRAYER
God, in this difficult situation,
we are thankful.

1 THESSALONIANS 5:18
Give thanks in all circumstances; for this
is God's will for you in Christ Jesus.

6.

LIVING WELL

He cuts off every branch in me that bears no fruit, while every branch that does bear fruit he prunes so that it will be even more fruitful.
—*John 15:2*

Weeks after the diagnosis, I was most afraid at night lying in bed, feeling the explosions inside my body, fasciculations popping. Twitching in my legs. Twitching in my back, pectoral muscles, everywhere. The twitching made me acutely aware of this war inside me—a fierce battle, that will eventually die out leaving a spent shell of skin and bones.

One night, after I drifted off to sleep, I dreamed I was at home with Kristin and the kids. "Do you want to come up to Daddy?" I asked Isaac. I couldn't lift him. I couldn't even move my arms. I dreamed I was in a wheelchair. My speech was slurred. I couldn't swallow. I had a feeding tube. Then, I dreamed I was paralyzed. I could only look around and blink. I couldn't breathe. I suffocated. Then, I died.

The dream was not a nightmare; I was not scared. Rather, I sensed it was a gift from God to deliver me, to liberate me from the fear of the future. I woke early the next morning well rested and free. I have nothing left to fear that I have not already faced. I had to lose my life before I could live.

It's not so bad dying when I have God and when I'm surrounded by the love and support of my family and friends. By comparison, the grief seemed worse in my early twenties when I lost my job and girlfriend. It was not what I lost, but rather that I wasn't prepared spiritually or emotionally to handle adversity. As for the job, I was miserable working there—a brutal work environment with high turnover. As for the girl, things were not going so well, and I had entertained the thought of breaking up with her, but she beat me to it. The grief stemmed from rejection.

I was mad and I was sad, at times vacillating between one and the other, but mostly mad and sad at the same time. I became intensely focused on bettering myself—on proving them wrong. I began an exercise routine. I worked out at the gym. I climbed the Stairmaster an hour every morning. Then I hit the trails to rollerblade around the Minneapolis Chain of Lakes for a couple hours every afternoon. I was not driven by discipline, but rather by escapism. Exercise numbed the pain. Also, I was accepted to the business school at the University of Minnesota. I needed to finish my degree. I applied myself to school with the same level of intensity as my exercise program and did quite well.

In spite of all the work to better myself on the outside, I didn't fix what was broken on the inside—the emptiness from not having a close connection with God and other Christians. It looked like I was handling life well, getting in shape and going to school, but I felt dead on the inside.

Now I'm facing adversity many times worse, but it seems manageable with a full life—a wonderful wife, great kids, and the support of friends and family. Most importantly, I have my faith that grounds me. I know that whatever happens in life, God will provide.

I wish God would go all the way and heal me, but if that is not His will, then I know He will at least give me the strength, mentally and spiritually, to get through this. I can already see His hand at work. I am thankful that God has given me my wife and kids, other family, and a Christian community. The timing of some events, like getting the diagnosis when my mother was surrounded by family, seemed like a God-thing. And He gave me that dream. He even gave me grief.

My grief was painful, but the answer wasn't to avoid the grief; it was to grieve well. Christ said, "Whoever wants to save his life will lose it, but whoever loses his life for me will save it" (Luke 9:24). He said that in a different context as he talked about following Him, but it applies here, too, in that I lost the life that I had—my health, my career, my dreams—and to find a new life, I needed to let go of what I had. My loss left something dead attached to me. My grief was the process of cutting off that dead thing, like pruning a dead branch off a tree so that the tree will grow to be healthy.

I understand there are several stages of grief, but I can never recall what they are, nor can I relate to them when I review them. I'm not interested in putting names to feelings. There were times over the first few months after the diagnosis when I desperately searched for another cause of my symptoms, but that gradually gave way to me accepting my fate. There were times of deep sadness, but other days seemed perfectly normal. Eventually, I came to have more normal days than sad days. I even came to see this disease as a blessing, in a way. Every one of us will die, some much sooner than others, and some more tragically than others. Some will have their lives snatched from them, leaving their family shocked. I, however, am on notice. I have time.

I have time to make sure that my son knows me, if not in person, then at least he will know my thoughts. I have time to tell my daughter, through my writing and by video, many of the things that a dad should say. I can help my wife through this grieving process. I can hold her while she cries as I whisper gently into her ear, "Grieve well."

Most importantly, I have time to build memories, to live well. My children will see a man who lived to his last breath. Though I have limited physical strength, I can demonstrate mental toughness. So much of life is out of my control, except for my attitude. Shouldn't this be how we all live, whether we have six years or sixty? I have decided to live well.

KRISTIN'S JOURNAL, JULY 2010: *Worry*

I can't handle thinking about the future. How will I raise two kids? How can we even plan when we don't know the timing? What am I going to do for a job? Should I go back to school? How would I pay for college? How will I pay for the kids' education? I was desperate to find a counselor to help me get a grip, so I called the biggest church in town. They sent me a list of recommended counselors. I scheduled an appointment.

In the first session, I described my overwhelming fear. The counselor explained that worry affects us physically: "God has not designed us to worry about the future, but to live in God's grace for today."

When my mind is focused on future possibilities or probabilities, my body responds as if it is my current reality—with anxiety. It's like a bad dream. It is not real, but my heart races because my body can't differentiate between reality and fantasy. When I watch an action movie, I am stressed right along with the characters to the point where I find myself praying for them. I then need to remind myself, "Kristin, this is not real."

The counselor said that we are not designed to know the future, to have a probable life expectancy. In our case, modern medicine has given us that. This disease is not like many others. With many other diseases, we would have hope, at least in the beginning, that perhaps we could beat it. With ALS, there is no treatment and no cure. We know how this is going to end. A hundred years ago, we would not have had this prognosis. Todd would have weak arms, but his probable future would not be mapped out. But we know his future, so we do need to plan as best we can—just not obsess about it.

I tried not to obsess. I put up a note by my kitchen sink that says, "Live with God's grace for today." I began to feel less anxious and fearful. However, when I wasn't stressed-out about the future, I was left with only my sadness. I want to keep my teammate and partner. When he buys me stamps, has the oil changed in the van, makes me breakfast, or plays with the kids, I think to myself, "I am going to miss him." Everything good today has this cloud hanging over it, Todd's diagnosis there in the back of my mind. I am grieving.

We can't control this disease, but we can control our response to it. Todd has chosen joy instead of anger and bitterness, and that makes it easier for me. If I am stressed, melting down and falling apart, that will be the reaction my kids will see, and they will follow my lead. We need to grieve, but we also need to be thankful for today's joys.

Today, I am thankful that Todd can pick up stamps, have my van's oil changed, and rub my back. I am thankful that today we went for a bike ride as a family. Tomorrow, we will find different joys for which to be thankful. I may not choose joy for my own sake, but I want to do it for Todd, because it will make his life better, and I especially want to do it for Sara and Isaac.

I tell myself, "So, Kristin, if you can't choose joy for yourself, then do it so Todd's remaining days and years won't be miserable. Do it so your kids can see how to live well, so they will grow up with a happy childhood."

God may use this for good in their lives, to give them empathy for people with disabilities and compassion for others. I am trying to trust God.

OUR PRAYER

God, help us to live with the grace You provide for today, rather than focusing on tomorrow's problems. You are our heavenly Father. You will take care of us.

MATTHEW 6:31–33 *So do not worry, saying, "What shall we eat?" or "What shall we drink?" or "What shall we wear?" For the pagans run after these things and your heavenly Father knows that you need them. But seek first his kingdom and his righteousness, and all these things will be given to you as well.*

7.

COMING TO ACCEPTANCE

"My grace is sufficient for you, for my power is made perfect in weakness."
—*2 Corinthians 12:9b*

It might have been denial, but I think it's normal, even diligent, to get another opinion. The first doctor I saw said this could be ALS, but he was a spine-care specialist. I then went straight to an ALS specialist. Because I hadn't seen other specialists, I thought that other possibilities may have been overlooked.

In August 2010, three months after my diagnosis, we traveled to the Mayo Clinic in Minnesota. Mayo takes an interesting approach. They review the medical history ahead of time and schedule the foreseen appointments contiguously, eliminating the need to drive back and forth to the clinic for various tests.

We drove to Rochester on a Sunday, a day early, and checked into a hotel. My Minnesota family took the opportunity to visit while I was in my home state. We had a family reunion of sorts. They were making an effort to see me. I felt loved.

I called my mother and told her that we had arrived. "Mom, you know, I won't be able to spend much time with you. They have me scheduled for two and a half solid days of appointments, and told me to stay an extra day in case I have more appointments."

"That's okay. We'll spend time with the kids."

The sun poured in as *a cappella* singers, perhaps Mennonite, filled the glass cavern with old hymns. The Mayo Clinic consists of two towers separated by a massive elevator bank fronted by a breathtaking atrium. We registered bright and early on Monday morning. My first appointment was with a movement disorder specialist, a neurologist who did *not* specialize in ALS.

We were called back to see the doctor and we waited in the exam room, which felt more like an office. The furniture was soft—a padded bench seat, like a couch, that ran alongside a desk. There was an examination table, but it didn't look clinical.

"I reviewed your medical records. They think you have ALS?"

"Yes, but I'm not so sure. I asked to see you because you are familiar with other disorders. I'm concerned that my diagnosis was premature, that I went to see an ALS specialist too soon." I asked him rhetorically, "You know the saying, to a carpenter, every problem looks like a nail?"

He chuckled. "I tell my students that all the time."

Kristin sat by me as I went through another round of pushing and prodding. The test was becoming all too familiar.

"I'm afraid to say that this looks like ALS. Your symptoms could not be explained by other disorders," he said, and my heart sank. "I see that you're scheduled for a series of tests. We should continue with those to make sure of the diagnosis. I also want to schedule you for another MRI, this one including a scan of your brain, to test for one other remote possibility."

After my appointments, we went to my aunt and uncle's house for dinner. My cousins were there along with my parents, siblings and a few of my uncle's friends. We sat on the deck in the backyard where my uncle was grilling hamburgers. My brother asked Kristin, "So, have you found out anything?"

"They think it's ALS," she said flatly.

His eyes widened.

"How will they treat that?" my uncle's friend asked.

"There's no treatment," I said.

"So then what will happen?"

"I will get weaker, then I will die."

"Oh!"

Over the next two days, I had blood tests, a urinalysis, a pulmonary test, an EMG and an MRI. I was scheduled to come back the next week for a follow-up appointment with the ALS specialist. It hardly seemed worth my while. I'd already seen an ALS specialist, and the non-ALS specialist didn't recognize this as anything else.

You'd think that managing a terminal disease would have been my priority, but I felt it was an inconvenience to go back to the Mayo Clinic. It seemed like my last hope was to have a non-ALS specialist find another explanation. *What good is it to talk to yet another ALS specialist?* I considered canceling the appointment, but decided instead to make lemonade out of the trip. I would take the opportunity to get answers to my questions, and then, after the appointment, I would golf with an old friend from Minneapolis.

I left Racine on a Wednesday morning at 5:00 a.m. and I drove five and a half hours across Wisconsin and into southern Minnesota to meet with Mayo's ALS specialist.

The doctor had reviewed my medical records ahead of time, so after introductions and pleasantries, he jumped into the same basic test. I knew it too well. "I agree with the doctor," he said, referring to the Mayo doctor I had seen the prior week. "This looks like ALS." And in the most gentle voice, he asked, "Do you have any questions?"

The doctor spent an hour and a half with me, answering one question after another. I came with a notebook and I was determined to understand this disease. I was glad that I had come back. Peace came over me. *Okay, I have ALS. Now what?*

He told me, "Progression is typically linear. If it starts slow, it will continue slow." Based on my self-assessment of strength a year ago, it seems I may be on the upper end of the bell curve relative to life expectancy. Although my breathing strength was at 50%, my forced vital capacity (lung function test) was still at 100%, and my swallowing was fine. My legs were still strong. All of the weakness seemed to be in my arms.

Nonetheless, the disease had progressed. One year prior, the only noticeable weakness was in my left bicep. I hadn't noticed much change even up to the original diagnosis, but over the summer, it became more difficult to type for long periods of time. Both hands fatigued after four to six hours of work. The specialist explained that I had reserve capacity and it only seemed sudden because the ALS had progressed to the point of noticing. It had been progressing all along.

Our hope that my diagnosis was all a big mistake was thoroughly dashed. After hearing it from four neurologists, I accepted that I have ALS. Coming to the point of full acceptance did not feel like giving up; rather, it felt like a burden lifted from my shoulders. Prior to the Mayo visit, I was reluctant to tell many people about my condition. After the Mayo visit, I became more open about it, and found that there were even more people willing to come along side me to help carry the burden.

We pray for healing, but we know the natural course of this disease, even of life. And although my body is weak, my spirit is strong.

"Hey, there's a problem. A car is parked in front of our house," Sara said, in early September, looking out the window. Then she paused and said, "It's not a problem. A problem is something that's hard to deal with."

It comes down to attitude. I've reflected on the past, in light of my condition, that I've worried about so much when there was really nothing to worry about, and now that I really have something to worry about, I haven't many worries.

In a strange way, it is liberating to have a terminal disease.

Kristin and I sat on the third floor porch of a beautiful condo overlooking Lake Delton while we vacationed in the Wisconsin Dells with my sister and her family. Kristin was journaling. Isaac woke up from his nap and she brought him to the porch and cuddled him on her lap. The sky was deep blue with puffy white clouds scattered about. Sara returned to the condo with Auntie, hungry for lunch after a couple hours in the pool.

On this day, there was no problem. We were learning to take life one day at a time.

KRISTIN'S JOURNAL, AUGUST 2010: *Anger*

I've never done much swearing. Leaving the county fair with my dad and two brothers when I was fifteen years old, and having just got my driver's permit, I really wanted to drive home. My dad told me I couldn't, and as I climbed into the backseat of the truck I snottily told him, "That really pisses me off."

My mild-mannered dad exploded, "What did you say?" I apologized. He said he didn't expect to hear such language from his little girl. We didn't swear in our household. It just wasn't done.

I used to cringe whenever I heard profanity in movies because I thought there were better ways to express one's feelings, until the diagnosis.

"Todd and I might write a book about our experience," I told my counselor.

"Well, don't think you have to have all the answers," he cautioned. "Something like this doesn't have easy answers, and, sometimes, Christians think they have to have it all figured out."

"Yeah, there might be too much swearing for it to be a Christian book anyway," I told him. "Sometimes swearing feels like the best expression of my anger about our situation. On Sunday, I worshiped in the morning and swore in the afternoon; it did not seem incongruent to me in my situation. I did both with my whole heart."

I am trying to adjust to life, but I am in a state of constant stress. Before I had Sara, I worked in an inner-city ministry. I have been thinking a lot about those kids I taught because many of them lived with stress and instability in their lives. Many lived on the brink of anger. If someone looked at them funny, bodies would bristle. If someone bumped into them, fists would fly.

I used to be a calm person, and it would take a lot to get to me. Now I am close to losing it all the time. My stress level is high. Isaac is not sleeping through the night, so neither am I. I snap in anger and I cry easily. God, help. Is this my new normal?

The only scripture that brings me hope right now is Psalm 88 and that is only because there is no hope in it. Other Psalms begin in despair, but, by the time they end, the author has climbed out of the miry pit, God has heard his cry and he is again praising God. In Psalm 88, the author stays in the pit.

I haven't been swearing at Todd or the kids or even at strangers in the grocery store who touch Isaac's face with their germy hands during flu season. I haven't cursed God, but I swear as I pray in desperation, "What are You doing God? This world is so messed up!" I am a little kid having a temper tantrum, pounding my feet, kicking and screaming to an unresponsive God, thankful that He can handle my anger.

I don't want to stay in this angry place forever. It is hard to be a decent mom and wife when I'm raging inside. I hope that someday I will get past Psalm 88 to Psalm 89, and like the author of that Psalm, praise God for His faithfulness.

OUR PRAYER

God, You want us to come to You in our desperation with honesty. God, work this anger out of us. Bring us to a better place.

PSALM 88: 1, 6, 14, & 18 *O Lord, the God who saves me, day and night I cry out to you. You have put me in the lowest pit, in the darkest depths. Why, O Lord, do you reject me and hide your face from me? You have taken my companions and loved ones from me; the darkness is my closest friend.*

8.

FINDING MY IDENTITY

But whatever was to my profit I now
consider loss for the sake of Christ.
—*Philippians 3:7*

Here will be times in your career when you'll be paid more than you're worth, and times when you'll be paid less," a mentor once told me. It is normal in my company for finance employees to rotate to different positions as they advance in management. A few years prior to the diagnosis, I landed a position that I wanted, but then after a couple years, I wanted to move on—to advance my career. I had a few interviews to rotate to different positions, but the jobs didn't come my way. I shrugged off each rejection thinking *next time*. Time was on my side.

In May 2010, I applied for my dream job. I began my career at the company in marketing research, and then transferred into a finance position. After holding two finance positions, there was an opening for a finance manager supporting marketing. The position would have employed my twin passions of marketing and finance and would have brought my career full circle. An interview was scheduled for June 15, which turned out to be four days after the diagnosis.

I didn't do well in the interview and they chose somebody else. I was almost as disappointed in hearing that I didn't get the job as when I first heard that I had ALS. It seems strange, I admit. Maybe I was so disappointed because I came face-to-face with the reality of what I was losing with ALS—time. It was my last opportunity, but I blew it, and then I ran out of time. It was like missing a lay-up at the buzzer when down by one point.

As I face this diagnosis, I grieve the end of my career. Unfulfilled, I have so much more to do, but no longer the time or ability. My identity is based, in part, on my career. Yes, I am also Kristin's husband and Sara's and Isaac's dad, but if I met somebody who should ask about me, I would likely tell that person where I work and what I do.

Eventually, I saw it as a blessing that I did not get the job. I was busy after the diagnosis, researching the disease, going to doctor appointments, and planning for my accelerated retirement. I was thankful to have a job that I knew well, where I could maintain a high level of performance with reduced hours and focus.

Then, in September 2010, as life started to seem normal again, albeit a new normal, an opportunity came along. I was offered a new role working outside of finance in manufacturing. The position, developing diagnostic and monitoring capabilities, was well-suited to my skills, and it came at a perfect time, as the reporting that was required in my finance job was getting too difficult for my weak hands to manage.

Fortunately, this disease has not yet affected my voice, so I can use speech-to-text dictation software and avoid using my hands for whatever typing that I do need to do in my current role.

A fellow person with ALS (PALS) told me, "It is best to go on disability when you are financially, emotionally and physically ready." I may be ready physically, but I am not there yet financially and emotionally. I'm fortunate to be working, and I truly enjoy every day that I work. I suppose I could go on disability now, but that time will come soon enough. We are meant to work, and while I can, I will.

I don't have any solution for coming to terms with the loss of a career. I just had to grieve.

It helped that I talked to people about it. As the words came out, I could hear how silly and self-centered I was. I had achieved more success in life than I deserve. I am not entitled to anything. There were two reasons to advance my career—the personal challenge and the recognition.

With my disability, I do not think I could have handled my dream job. I wouldn't have even enjoyed it. I could even view this as God's protective hand closing that door, knowing what is best for me.

As for the recognition, it doesn't matter much to me anymore if I'm recognized for being anything other a wonderful husband, a great dad, and a follower of Christ. I would have wasted my life if all people saw in me was the hollow shell of a career.

A diagnosis like ALS has a way of putting life into perspective. I enjoy my work now, challenged to make the most of my time and ability, content with my current position. I am learning to find my identity as a citizen of heaven, eagerly awaiting my Savior. (Philippians 3:20)

KRISTIN'S JOURNAL, SEPTEMBER 2010:
Where Is the Hope?

Will I dream again? I experience bursts of happiness as I appreciate life and the time we have, but I am not enthused for the future. Things are going to get worse, and they may not get better until Heaven.

On a crisp fall day, my neighbor Jana called me to see if I wanted to go for a walk with her and her daughters. Jana and I are kindred spirits as we both grew up in the country and neither of us knows pop culture; Todd joked that I was born forty years too late and Jana, a hundred. We often meet and walk in the cemetery in our neighborhood.

Jana's daughter and Sara rode their bikes in front of us while we pushed the younger ones in strollers.

"I have been researching earth-sheltered homes," Jana told me. "Tim and I would like to build one someday." I am often intrigued by the ideas my free-spirited friend comes up with. Later, I looked it up on-line to see what she was talking about. One couple built their cave-like home themselves using gnarled branches and earth. They nicknamed it The Hobbit House.

Todd and I used to have dreams too. He was hoping to advance his career, maybe relocate. We looked forward to traveling with our children to national parks and overseas. The specific dreams were not important to me, but rather that we dreamed, and that they were our dreams—Todd and I together, with our children in this adventure of life. When Todd was diagnosed, our dreams died.

I have the hope of Heaven, but what about hope for the rest of my life on this earth? The context of the frequently quoted verse, Jeremiah 29:11—"'For I know the plans I have for you,' declares the Lord, 'plans to prosper you and not to harm you, plans to give you hope and a future.'"—is God bringing His people out of captivity. It was a promise of earthly hope.

When I took urban ministry classes in college, I learned about the importance of hope. Many people who live in the inner city don't have hope for the future and that contributes to the cycle of poverty and despair. I want hope now, for this earth. And I want Todd, my best friend, here to parent Sara and Isaac with me.

I am grieving the loss of the future I dreamed of, and trying to figure out how to embrace the future that is coming.

OUR PRAYER

God, we don't look forward to the future this disease will bring. Give us the strength to persevere, grow our character, and produce hope in our lives. Help us to trust You with our present and our future.

ROMANS 5:2b-3 *And we rejoice in the hope of the glory of God. Not only so, but we also rejoice in our sufferings, because we know that suffering produces perseverance; perseverance, character; and character, hope. And hope does not disappoint us, because God has poured out his love into our hearts by the Holy Spirit, whom he has given us.*

9.

GETTING A GRIP ON SELF-PITY

In all these things we are more than conquerors through him who loved us.
—*Romans 8:37*

Oh, God, please let it be me instead," I'd plead if my child were sick. Well, it is me, and my children are healthy. A few months after the diagnosis, and after having been to Mayo for a third and fourth opinion, I called my dear, old friend Anka. The call was difficult to make; I had been procrastinating because these calls were awkward. They usually began with "How are you? What's new with you?" But it is hard to get right to the point: "Oh, not much, I have a terminal disease."

On this call, my "How are you?" was replied with, "I wish I could say well."

It had been a tough summer for Anka's beautiful, eight-year-old Rebecca. She was born with a heart condition that the doctors tried to correct with several surgeries. But her heart was failing. The conversation eventually came around to me, which in light of little Becca, seemed trivial.

I appreciate the outpouring of love and support from friends and family, and the affirmation when told how unfair this is because I am so nice. (People seem much nicer with the realization that they're dead or dying.) But I really do not feel it is unfair for me. It is unfair for my wife, my children and my parents. As for me, I've lived a full life. I had a great childhood, all thirty years of it. I achieved success in my career. I married a beautiful, loving woman. I've had the opportunity to tuck my daughter into bed, tell her a dream, and pray with her. I've shushed and rocked my crying son to sleep.

Anka told me that Rebecca was braver than she. Rebecca did not fear the future. As a child of God, I need not fear death, either. Oh, I dread the process of getting there, but as for death itself, I welcome it.

Years earlier, Anka and I attended college at the University of Minnesota. We became fast friends at the business school where she and I were a few years older than the average student. We would work on group projects at her house, which allowed her to watch her son, and I became quite fond of her family—her husband, son, and parents.

She knew of my faith in Christ, so she asked me one day after I told her that I had attended my grandmother's funeral, "Why aren't you afraid to die? Why aren't Christians afraid to die?"

I explained that death has lost its sting. I explained that I had already died in Christ, and that now my home is in Heaven. "Heaven is a better place, and I look forward to it."

I spoke those words when death seemed abstract. I had my whole life ahead of me. Death was so far away that it seemed nothing to be feared, whether one believed in Christ or not.

In November, Becca had a heart transplant, which means that another family plunged into unimaginable grief. A beautiful gift had been given to a beautiful girl.

Anka called me because Becca wanted to speak to me. She had told Becca that I was a man of God and that I was praying for her, and that it was a miracle that she was doing so much better now. Becca wanted to thank me. "I am sorry to hear about you. My mom told me you are sick," she said, and my eyes welled up with tears and I felt a lump in my throat.

I told her, "You and I have a special bond. We've both faced death. We've stared it down. You are a fighter, Rebecca, and I am so proud of you."

What good could possibly come of a little girl with a bad heart? What good could possibly come of my ALS?

After a few months of seeing a chiropractor for my "pinched nerve" and not getting improvement, Kristin made an appointment with another chiropractor in the area who specialized in neuropathy. I began seeing Dr. Jay after the spine-care specialist first intimated that I might have ALS, but before the ALS neurologist confirmed it.

Dr. Jay was patient and thorough. He knew that he would not be able to cure ALS, but we were still open to other possible causes and treatments. He was compassionate, and he was genuinely interested in my health. He gave me hope during a time when I would have otherwise been hopeless.

Hearing of my diagnosis in June 2010, Dr. Jay showed empathy typically hidden by healthcare professionals. He asked if he could put my name in the offering basket for prayer at his church. He confided that he had been thinking about his life and how he would deal with such news. His wife was pregnant with their first child at the time. I continued to see him for a few months after the diagnosis. I was not ready to accept it, and his treatments seemed to help. The treatments included stretching, which, I would later learn, keeps my muscles limber.

One evening, I saw Dr. Jay help somebody into his car. He then attached a wheelchair to a carrier, like a bike carrier strapped to the trunk. I watched, curiously, wondering if it was his brother. They looked alike.

On my next visit I asked Dr. Jay whom he was helping. The man was his friend, Bobby, who has a rare genetic disorder in his brain that caused his muscles to permanently contract. I forget the name of the condition. I haven't heard of it before, nor had most doctors; it took years to get a diagnosis. Dr. Jay showed me a picture of himself and Bobby, when they were about eight years old, in their little league baseball caps and uniforms. Bobby started showing symptoms not long after that picture was taken. The disease has taken a toll on Bobby, and it greatly impacted his best friend Jay.

"Is that why you went into chiropractic care?" I asked.

"Yes. But ironically, Bobby's condition is well beyond the scope of my training." Dr. Jay said.

God worked for good, through that situation, to give this world a passionate and compassionate caregiver. I struggle in trying to understand God's hand in this. God is sovereign, but does He really pick this one for ALS at age thirty-nine or that one for heart failure at age eight? Surely, He has the power to stop disease and death, so He must have allowed it. Why? I don't know, but the Word says that in all things, God works for the good of those who love Him.

I used to say, "There is nothing good about what I have, except for knowing there are things worse." But I can see that there can be good in it, not in the disease, per se, but in what can come of the disease, if I allow God to use me. As part of the body of Christ, I can show that there can be joy and peace even in the midst of sorrow. I can model for others, especially for my children, a godly response to adversity. How will He use this for good for Sara and Isaac? Will God give them compassion beyond what I've ever felt? Will He give them a passion for something, building on this experience?

Being a Christian does not mean we are protected from all the troubles of life. Being a Christian means that when faced with adversity we can turn to God, who will work for our good.

KRISTIN'S JOURNAL, SEPTEMBER 2010:
It Is a Journey

The sermon at church today was about how the Bible is the playbook for dealing with situations. The Holy Spirit and the Word teach us how we can be successful. I sat there thinking, "I am feeling a little stuck here and I'm not alone. I read the Psalms and in many of them David is depressed, thinking that God has forsaken him. Well, I am depressed. Where's the success?"

Then during the worship music, as I was singing, "Thank You for the cross my friend," it hit me. I can be thankful for this cross, too—not that I want Todd to have ALS or want my kids to grow up without a dad. I love Todd and this is not what I want or choose, but I can be thankful for what the ALS is doing in our spiritual lives.

I was in a comfortable place before the diagnosis, and I often thought about how I was becoming fond of my life: my pretty bungalow, my nice new wool rug, my mini-van, and money to take vacations. Success! But God's definition of success is something different; it is His character produced in us, in our hearts and in the hearts of our children.

So that's where I was during church: encouraged, surrendered, and worshiping. By lunch time, I had fallen from such a lofty place. I had PMS. I was irritable and argumentative with my family. I cried as I told Todd about my relapse and he said, "So you thought you were Elisabeth Elliot, but found out you were really Tammy Faye Baker."

I was tired, cranky, and angry. I wanted my low-stress, happy life back, or else I wanted to crawl in bed and read Jan Karon novels and escape to Mitford.

Sara witnessed our arguments today and asked me, "Why are you so crabby, Mom?"

"I don't know," I snapped. I saw the crushed look on her face. "Come, and give me a hug. I'm sorry I was crabby." I apologized to Todd for being cranky, and then had a talk with God: "God, I don't think this is a good way for me to live, years of knowing my husband is dying. I don't think it is a good plan for our lives and I'm angry."

I am angry at the thought of losing the father of my children and my best friend. Life is hard now, but it will be so much harder when he is gone. I pray that this will be slow and that we will have many years together. But when it gets to the point where Todd is miserable, when Todd feels his quality of life has deteriorated to the point that he'd rather be with Christ in heaven, I hope that part is short. Todd and I were talking about this the other night. He is concerned that he may be really uncomfortable for years.

This is going to be a hard, long journey, because every time Todd progresses there will be new challenges and more grief. I talked on the phone to a woman whose husband died from ALS twenty-two months after the diagnosis. She shared her story with me two years after her husband's death and she cried as she talked about it. "I haven't cried about this for a long time," she said.

If this is what is to be, I want this to be as long as possible. At the same time, I know it will be hard and sad and I know I won't finish grieving until well after it is all over. I think I will cry about this until it is over, and then I will cry some more, and then not as often. But hopefully, we will have fifteen years of this joy and sadness.

OUR PRAYER

God, we are on a journey that
puts life into perspective.

ECCLESIASTES 7:2 *It is better to go to a house of mourning than to go to a house of feasting. For death is the destiny of every man; the living should take this to heart.*

10.

APPRECIATING LIFE

Command those who are rich in this present world not to be arrogant nor to put their hope in wealth, which is so uncertain, but to put their hope in God, who richly provides us with everything for our enjoyment.
—*1 Timothy 6:17*

Huck Finn had the river. I had the lake and the Great North Woods. I canoed and motor-boated on Swan Lake, right out the back door of my childhood home. I mini-biked in the thousands of acres of abandoned iron mining property across the road. I climbed an abandoned crane. I walked electric fences with my friend on his dad's hobby farm. I hunted for grouse, driving the trails in my friend's Delta Eighty-Eight, shotguns on the hood, until we would either see game or the trail became too narrow for that wide boat. And I hunted deer with my brother-in-law John and my cousin Greg.

A short time after the diagnosis, Greg called. He didn't know what to say, which is understandable, but he wanted to reconnect. He suggested that we go deer hunting in November. Greg and I were more than cousins; we were best friends. I grew up with Greg, even though we were separated by two hundred miles. We spent time at each other's house every summer. He lived near Minneapolis, wishing he was a country boy. I lived in northern Minnesota, loving the excitement of the city. When we were old enough, we began to hunt. I taught Greg how to hunt grouse. We taught ourselves how to hunt deer. We walked around the woods as if expecting a deer to pop out in front of us on the trail. John eventually taught us to scout the property looking for rubbings and trails, and then build stands high in the trees. Greg continued to hunt with John, but I was too busy with school and work, then moved out of state, so I hadn't hunted for years.

I was excited to relive my childhood, but apprehensive because I wasn't sure how far the disease would progress come November and if I'd be able to hold a gun. Also, I didn't know if I'd be able to take time off work, as deer hunting season would've fallen over month-end close, a time when I had many accounting and reporting responsibilities at work. John loved the idea of me hunting with him and wanted to make sure that I didn't have any excuse to back out, so he paid for the license and he bought a hunting blind—a tent with holes in the side—so I wouldn't need to climb a tree. And, as if God wanted me to go, I ended up transferring to a different position at work, so no longer had the conflict of month-end close. As November approached, the disease had not progressed much, so the hunting trip was on and Kristin and I made a family vacation out of it; Kristin and the kids came along to visit my parents.

I brought warm clothes, prepared for subfreezing weather as is typical in November, but it ended up being unseasonably warm so I enjoyed time by the lake with Sara. We built a bonfire and roasted marshmallows and I pointed out the constellations to her. But the warm weather meant that hunting would be bad, as the deer were not in rut. I did not mind because, for me, deer hunting was not about shooting a deer. I am not sure I would have known what to do if I had. I just wanted to spend time with John and Greg. Hunting is the best kind of time to spend with other guys, which is to say we talk at breakfast, lunch and dinner, but otherwise ignore each other all day—except for an occasional text message—as we sit hundreds of yards apart.

We woke early on Saturday morning to post before sunrise. Greg outfitted me with a blaze-orange jacket, John provided a gun with a scope (my old Marlin 30-30 is a brush gun, not adequate for the field I would sit in), and John set up a tent for me alongside the field. I set up my spotting scope—it is safer to use that than the scope on the gun—and looked around the field and at Venus rising in the horizon. I practiced how I would hold the gun if I happened to see a deer. I didn't have enough strength with my left arm to hold the gun up, so I zipped up the windows on the tent high enough so that the sides of the tent could be used to support the gun. Then I sat alone with my thoughts.

The prior November, my left bicep was weak, but I had enough muscle elsewhere to compensate, and I did not think I was dying. Nothing physically changed after the diagnosis, but hearing that I had a life expectancy of three to five years changed my whole world. "We better enjoy the summer," I told Kristin after the diagnosis, "because this may be the best it gets." Things did get better though, not physically, but in my mind I returned to a new normal, enjoying life again.

As I sat in the tent with windows opened to the North, South and East, I heard a deer walk through the woods on the west side of the tent. I inched the zippered window open. The noise in the woods stopped as the deer must've heard the mechanical sound, then it walked on. I could hear snapping branches, but could not see through the dense brush. I sent a text message to the other guys. "See anything?" John replied that he saw a deer walk out of the woods from behind my tent and then walk across the field. The deer was over a ridge from where I could see it, and too far for John to take a shot. Ten minutes later, we heard a shot ring out from a half mile east. Somebody on the far side of the field shot it—an eight point buck, we later found out. Although that was the only thing seen or heard, I had fun.

As a father, I long for my children to experience the pleasure of my childhood, and it was especially so after the diagnosis. My childhood was filled with grand adventures: canoeing up the O'Brien Creek, portaging beaver dams, then finding a grassy point bar on which to rest and have a snack. Some kids do those things at summer camp, but I lived it every day. I didn't just read about the adventures of Huckleberry Finn; I lived them. Those experiences shaped who I am today. Perhaps, if Sara and Isaac can have similar experiences when we move to the Upper Peninsula, they will know me better and that will be part of my legacy.

KRISTIN'S JOURNAL, NOVEMBER 2010: *Surrender*

Sometimes things get worse before they get better. When the insurance handbook came out for the upcoming year, we noticed a change to the long-term disability coverage: neuromuscular disorders will only be eligible for twenty-four months of coverage, rather than through retirement age. After two years on disability, Todd's employment from the company would be severed and the life insurance benefit would go away.

I felt so stressed at the thought of trying to provide for two kids. I was a basket-case again, thinking, "What will happen next? Will one of my kids get sick and die? Will I get cancer?" I had a headache and my stomach was all knotted up. I felt like giving up. "Take us to Heaven now, God. Do You hate us, God?" I could relate to Naomi in the book of Ruth: "It grieves me very much for your sakes that the hand of the LORD has gone out against me! ...Call me Mara for the Almighty has dealt very bitterly with me." (Ruth 1: 13b and 20b NKJV) I was angry.[6] "Those benefits were one thing we were thankful for in our difficult situation and now they are going away. God, this stinks."

After more tears and angry prayers, I realized that I cannot have confidence in anything but God—not in my plans, finances, health, or the promise of tomorrow—and, with that realization, I surrendered. "God, this is out of my control. God, I need You. There are no other guarantees in life." The anxiety, stress, worry and fear subsided when I gave up trying to control my life, when I came to God with my broken heart.

In hard times, I am more desperate, and desperation brings me to God. We all experience hard things. We can dull our desperation with TV, the Internet, alcohol, shopping, or fun while we wait for things to get better. Or, we can come to God. I am in that place this morning desperately worshiping. I probably won't stay here. (I know myself too well.) But, for now, this is a good place to be.

Todd got clarification of the benefits the following week and found out that ALS is still covered—only certain neuromuscular conditions that do not result in paralysis are restricted to two years, which is an industry standard—so I was again thankful for those benefits. But my attitude changed. I am not clinging so tightly to those benefits as my hope.

OUR PRAYER

God, only in You can we put our hope. Only in You can we trust.

PSALM 62:5-6 *Find rest, O my soul, in God alone; my hope comes from him. He alone is my rock and my salvation; he is my fortress, I will not be shaken.*

11.

FIGHTING

Do you not know that your body is a temple
of the Holy Spirit, who is in you, whom
you have received from God? You are not
your own; you were bought with a price.
Therefore honor God with your body.

—*1 Corinthians 6:19–20*

I ache at the thought of Kristin losing her husband (not to mention that I am that husband.) The least I owe her is to try to extend my life as long as possible. Back when I thought I would live to be an old man, I felt that my diet was none of Kristin's concern. I ate the healthy food she put in front of me, but I didn't go out of my way to avoid any food she would consider unhealthy. I am now listening to Kristin, as we've adopted an all-of-the-above approach to managing my health. We will do everything we can within reason.

I've been able to learn many things in life—miscellaneous facts like Fahrenheit to Celsius conversions and word etymologies. But there is this whole knowledge-base of natural remedies, supplements, and dietary lifestyles that my wife is tuned into but of which I have no ability to grasp. Kristin and her mother, Lani, would say such things as, "*They* say you should take beta carotene if your eyes are dry."

I would challenge them, "Who are *they*?"

After the diagnosis, I was ready to listen to *them*. I went on a gluten-free, low-dairy, low-sugar, semi-organic diet, and I did feel better. I eventually became more sensitive to taste, and I could tell the difference between regular eggs and free-range eggs from antibiotic-free hens. They look different and they taste different.

To optimize my health, my favorite deodorant was banned as it contained aluminum. *They* say aluminum is a neuro-toxin. I have seen no evidence that it does any harm, but with my neuromuscular system compromised, I did not want to take any chances. Kristin bought a salt stick from our local health-food store. After a few weeks of using it, the salt stick did not get any smaller, I developed a rash, and I could hardly stand the smell of myself. One day, in desperation, I pulled out my reserve aluminum deodorant. I didn't get three steps into the kitchen before Kristin called me on it. (Kristin has an amazing nose. I joke that she could work for the police K-9 unit… without a dog.)

Kristin went into action and called the natural remedy help-line, her mother. Kristin informed me that a good natural deodorant is vodka. I asked, "I'm supposed to drink vodka?"

"No, you splash it under your arms."

I had visions of being pulled over by the police. "Offither," speech slurred under this dreaded condition, "it'th my deodorant." Then the officer would ask me to get out and walk a straight line. *Oh great.*

I sent Kristin back to the health food store to look for another aluminum-free deodorant option.

At a business dinner with a group of colleagues, I learned that my colleague Wendy was on a raw, vegan diet. She ate only raw, uncooked vegetables and nuts. She went on the diet because she wasn't able to digest meat and other cooked foods.

She said it wasn't hard to go on the diet because the alternative was "praying to the porcelain god."

I told her, "I would be bored out of my mind for several hours if you ever got together with my wife." They would go on and on talking about what *they* say.

Wendy explained how she could make anything raw, including lasagna with sliced zucchini and ground macadamia nuts for cheese. She could make a German chocolate cake with raw chocolate. She shared with me a raw chocolate truffle, which, I have to admit, was quite delicious.

I asked Wendy about her dogs. She reminded me that they were mutts, rottweiler coloring but smaller. I asked, "Like dachshunds?"

"No. The dogs are fifty pounds," Wendy said.

"You buy the eighty pound bags of dog food?" another co-worker asked with a chuckle.

Wendy's eyes widened in surprise. "Oh, no, they eat what I eat."

"Raw vegetables?" I asked.

"Yeah. They eat fruit and vegetables. I give them the ends of carrots and the other scraps. There's nothing that goes to waste in our house. They eat all the vegetables except lettuce; dogs won't eat leaves. I buy them raw hamburger and chicken too. When the dogs were two, they were really unhealthy and we had a lot of vet bills. Now they look great."

"Did they go on the raw diet first, or did you?" I asked.

"I went on the diet first. Then I figured if it works for me it should work for them," she said, as if it was the most logical thing to do.

"My wife wants me to eat something raw at every meal," I contributed as if part of the club. "She juices vegetables for me every morning. I drink a glass of carrot juice, usually with something else in it like kale or spinach."

Another co-worker, Josh, jumped into the conversation, "Kale is really tough. It gets hot when you juice it."

"We have a twin gear juicer," I bragged.

"My dogs love the carrot pulp from the juicer," Wendy said.

Josh explained that he purchased food from a cooperative. He said the food tasted so much better. I affirmed his opinion. "Are you on an organic diet?" he asked me.

"We are really only on an organic diet for the dirty dozen." He looked puzzled, at which point Wendy jumped in by rattling off the list.

"We don't buy everything organic," I said. "I cannot tell the difference in the taste of the bananas."

"My dogs can. They won't eat non-organic bananas or strawberries," Wendy said. "I had somebody dog-sit for me once. They said, 'Your dogs don't drink much water.' I asked them what kind of water they were feeding them. They said, 'Tap.' I said, 'They drink filtered water.' So I poured them filtered water and they drank like they hadn't drunk for a week."

There is a spectrum. I am eating more organics, but all things considered, I am still pretty normal.

There is no cure for ALS and nothing has been shown to significantly extend life. However, I can manage the symptoms and improve my quality of life.

I take supplements to control cramping, aid digestion, and optimize my health. We purchased a massage table and Kristin massages my muscles every night to keep them limber. And we are trying other things, whether they will help or not, because I have nothing to lose.

Studies have shown that there is a placebo effect. It is good for my soul and body to try something. To give up and go home to die seems so hopeless. As long as we do no harm, why not at least try? I plan to die in the best health of my life.

KRISTIN'S JOURNAL, NOVEMBER 2010:
Winning

On a warm October Saturday, the day before Halloween, we went trick-or-treating at the zoo. Sara dressed as Mary Poppins and Isaac as a penguin, like in the Jolly Holiday scene. Sara came up with the idea. Isaac had just learned to walk a couple months prior, so he waddled through the zoo like a penguin. We stopped to ride the carousel, which was fitting, as Mary Poppins rode on one in that scene. We took a lot of pictures.

We ran into another couple dressed as Bert, Dick Van Dyke's character, and a penguin. It inspired us to turn Todd into Bert the following day, for the actual day of Halloween. We created a cardboard top hat and striped Todd's sport-jacket with red electrical tape. On Sunday, we went trick-or-treating in the neighborhood; Mary Poppins holding Bert's hand, followed by the waddling penguin. The weekend was magical, just living life.

Monday came and Todd was wiped out, his legs stiff and sore. I was so happy he had the opportunity to dress up and go trick-or-treating with the kids, but sad that it was so physically hard on him. I was hopeful that this disease would not progress past his arms, but I now see his legs are affected by moderate—not even moderate, but minimal—physical activity. At this rate, he could very well need a wheelchair by next year.

I feel sad for my kids, for what will be normal for them. "I want Sara and Isaac to feel like they are in a secure world," I told my counselor. "I want to protect them from pain."

"You can't protect them from pain," he said, "but you can prepare them to go through pain. Your life doesn't measure up to your original plan. Your kids might get bitter and rebellious, but other kids do too. It is your life, and you need to deal with it as it is. That doesn't mean you approve, like, or agree with it. It is what it is."

"I want to fight this disease," I told him. "I want to at least try alternative therapies that won't do harm: supplements, juicing, and nightly massage."

"If you are fighting, then how do you define winning?" he asked.

I pondered the question, then the answer came, "Fighting is winning. We win if we do not give up."

We are working to optimize Todd's health—digestion supplements, antioxidants, minerals, vitamins and nightly massage. We are trying everything within reason; we don't want to spend money foolishly. Trying something, even if there is no scientific proof that it helps, is better than doing nothing. And doing something helps me; it keeps me from feeling helpless.

Besides, we know that at least some of what we are doing actually helps Todd feel better. Todd's muscles cramp less when he is taking his supplements. He walks less stiffly after a good massage.

For the week after Halloween, I gave Todd extra supplements and long massages. He eventually recovered back to his new normal.

OUR PRAYER
God, help us prepare our children
to face a pain-filled world.

DEUTERONOMY 6:6-7 *These commandments that I give you today are to be upon your hearts. Impress them on your children. Talk about them when you sit at home and when you walk along the road, when you lie down and when you get up.*

12.

KNOWING
THE FUTURE

Who of you by worrying can add
a single hour to his life?
—*Matthew 6:27*

The first time I couldn't climb stairs was fifteen years ago, long before the disease, or at least long before the disease had any measurable impact. I did not think I was dying that Monday morning when I could not walk up the stairs to my office. Looking back now, the experience provides understanding of how this disease affects my muscles.

On a crisp, colorful, autumn Saturday, in an old-growth forest, I played paintball with my co-workers. I am not a militia man by any means, so I did not have much sense but to run through the woods trying to capture the flag only to get pelted with hard-on-a-cold-day paintballs. Those balls stung when they hit my exposed neck, and they'd leave a hickey, something odd peeking out from the collar of the suit and tie I was required to wear at work.

After a few games on offense, I was exhausted and chose to take up a position defending the flag. I had learned it was best to wait until the guys were nearly on top of me before opening fire. Exchanging volleys from thirty yards away wasted pellets; I would eventually run out of ammo and they would storm the fort. In one game, I waited for my co-worker Rufus to sneak all the way up to the flag. Probably thinking the guard had gotten bored and run off, he grabbed the flag, turned around, and THOOMP! I shot him in the butt from five yards away. He got huffy, cursed and stomped away like a little kid. Rufus made me laugh as he feigned indignation with a slight smirk.

After mentioning Rufus, I can't resist telling another story about him. There were six analysts that sat in a cubicle area no larger than the office I sit in now. We called it the pen and we played practical jokes on each other. One day, Rufus left his computer unattended. I edited his e-mail options to auto correct Rufus to Doofus. (You know when you type something like "beleive" and the computer changes it automatically to "believe?") Well, every time Rufus sent an e-mail and tried to sign off Rufus, it came out Doofus. He was so mad.

Anyway, after playing paintball on that Saturday, I was exhausted, but satisfied. I laid low on Sunday. On Monday morning, I could barely roll out of bed. I walked down the stairs of my apartment, stiff but able. I drove the twenty minutes to my office, feeling my muscles ache. I walked stiffly across the parking lot and into the building.

As I started up the grand staircase to my cubicle on the second floor, I could not climb the stairs, my muscles being so fatigued I could not lift my own weight up seven inches to mount the first step. I took the elevator. I knew I overdid it, but I had no anxiety because I was young and healthy, and my muscles would recover and be left stronger.

Now, my muscles are like a bad battery on a cell phone: There's only enough power to make a few calls a day, so I best choose which calls I want to make. I can only plug in my phone at night to recharge it, and every day the phone will carry less and less of a charge.

I am weak. There is pain when my muscles cramp, on occasion, but most of the time I am just weak. In the beginning stages, when upper motor neurons that control certain muscles start to die, those muscles get stiff and sore if overworked. Then, when the lower motor neurons die, the affected muscles fatigue, leaving me with no strength at all. It does not take a day of paintball to get to that point. Typing all day at work so fatigues my hands that feeding myself in the evening is difficult.

In January 2011, we attended our second ALS clinic—*our* clinic, as ALS is a disease that hits families, not just individuals. Every PALS in the waiting room was accompanied by somebody. Looking around the lobby, one African American fellow, perhaps fifty years old, was in a wheelchair. His arms and legs were motionless and much too thin. His head was in a brace to keep his chin up. Another man, a white guy with an eighties-style mullet, was with a twenty-something woman, perhaps his daughter. His speech was slurred, but when they called for him, he stood up and shuffled to the door. Though I know the future will be difficult, I cannot assume I will progress like anybody else; this disease takes a different path for everybody.

A nurse called us back into Exam Room 1, the same room where I first received my diagnosis. First, a pulmonary nurse checked my forced vital capacity—my ability to expel air from my lungs. I scored ninety-four percent, but my reduced lung capacity may have been due to a slight cold. Then other specialists—nutritionist, occupational therapist, physical therapist, and social worker—paraded in and out of our room checking on the state of my health, answering questions, and providing information they thought we might need to know, but did not know to ask. I explained my difficulty buttoning my pants, not due to the lack of dexterity, but because my left arm was too weak to draw my pants together. I had the most trouble after my pants were freshly washed, exacerbated by my morning routine. Showering, drying, shaving, brushing and all that other stuff fatigued my arms. The occupational therapist gave me a tool that looked like a device to thread needles, but ten times larger. It goes through the button hole and hooks around the button.

After a few minutes, the doctor came in and conducted an abbreviated version of the very familiar exam. He pushed and pulled on my arms and wrote down numbers. It had been over six months since my diagnosis.

I was interested in the scores assigned to my strength based on the doctor's objective, unbiased opinion. Having had a ten-year career in marketing research, I did not want to bias the observer, so I wasn't forthcoming when he first asked if I'd been having difficulties. "Is it difficult turning over in bed?"

"No."

"Is your writing becoming more sloppy?" he asked.

"Well," I answered, as if perplexed, "my writing is always sloppy."

My scores in my already-weak left hand were about the same. The scores in my right hand and arm were a tad lower. My shoulders had lost strength. My legs were still strong. In my case, progression meant the loss of function measured month by month, rather than week by week.

The truth is that I had been having more difficulty than I let on. I could turn over in bed fine, but I had trouble pulling the heavy blanket up to my chin. My writing was no more sloppy than normal, but I couldn't write for more than a few minutes. I had planned to write journals for Kristin, Sara, and Isaac, but then I realized I could not write more than a page at a time.

Clinic was difficult because I am not that interested in

knowing the future. I had trouble shaking the images of those people in the waiting room knowing that my days ahead would be harder. The future will be harder than today; I'd rather live in today.

KRISTIN'S JOURNAL, JANUARY 2011:
Pleading

Today, at our second ALS clinic, I discreetly observed the other patients. One man could still walk but had a neck collar. There was a man who walked crookedly and stiffly. I saw a man who had no problem sitting up, but he was in a wheelchair. Then, there was a man in a wheelchair who was really thin, had a neck collar, and his hands and arms hung limply. Todd was one of the youngest ones there. I was upset seeing what this disease does to people. I watched Todd walk up to the desk. He was walking a little stiffly.

We went out for dinner with friends the other night. Our friend asked God to bless our meal and he prayed, praising God for being so great. I don't feel like praising God for how wonderful He is lately. My prayers are more pleading, "Please, God, heal Todd. Thank You for getting us through this, but You are God, You can heal Todd. Yet You haven't."

How I feel toward God reminds me of how I felt toward my parents when I was a young teenager. Although I knew they loved me, I didn't like their rules for my life. I have a passage of scripture memorized, "My son, do not make light of the Lord's discipline, and do not lose heart when he rebukes you, because the Lord disciplines those he loves, and he punishes everyone he accepts as a son. Endure hardship as discipline; for God is treating you as sons. For what son is not disciplined by his father?" (Hebrews 12:5b-7) I know God loves me, but I don't like this plan for my life.

The Bible teaches us to be persistent in prayer. God wants us to be like the annoying neighbor who keeps coming to your door asking for bread. I don't understand this parable, because I don't like it when Sara whines or repeatedly asks for things. In fact, I tell her, "You already asked me. I said, 'No.' Now I don't want to hear any more about it." I intentionally do not give in when she asks repeatedly because I don't want to encourage that behavior.

I feel at odds with God. I want Him to do something He is not doing. Jesus did not want to go to the cross, and He pleaded with his Father, but then He submitted and said, "Not as I will, but as you will." (Matt. 26:39b) I plead with God to heal Todd, and then I submit to this situation only because that's the way things are and I can't change them. My submission doesn't result in warm feelings toward God.

"What is the point of being persistent in prayer? Isn't God going to do what He is going to do anyway?" I asked Jana.

"Obedience," she replied.

Well, I am being obedient in persistently praying for healing for Todd. "God, we know You can heal. Please heal Todd."

What is the point of our suffering? Jesus prayed that the cup of suffering would be taken from Him, but at least He knew the purpose. Jana tells me we need to trust that there is a purpose, even if we may never know it.

It is devastating to deal with a terminal disease for which there is no treatment or cure. I think about Bible times with the lack of modern medicine. There weren't a lot of treatments or cures. "Jesus, Son of David, have mercy on me!" a blind beggar called out (Luke 18:38b) and Jesus healed him.

"Lord, if you are willing, you can make me clean," a leper said, as he worshiped (Luke 5:12b).

"'I am willing,' Jesus said. 'Be clean.' And immediately the leprosy left him" (Luke 5:13b). In the days of Jesus, sick people were desperate people. Oftentimes, today, we are not as desperate because we have things under control with modern medicine. Tylenol for a fever. Surgery. With ALS, medicine doesn't have the answer, so there is desperation. I pray, "Jesus, if You are willing, heal Todd."

OUR PRAYER

God, we pray with persistence that You would perform a miracle and heal. God, bring us to the point where we pray like Jesus, "not as I will, but as You will."

LUKE 11:5-10 *[Jesus] said to [His disciples,] "Suppose one of you has a friend, and he goes to him at midnight and says, 'Friend, lend me three loaves of bread, because a friend of mine on a journey has come to me, and I have nothing to set before him.' "Then the one inside answers, 'Don't bother me. The door is already locked, and my children are with me in bed. I can't get up and give you anything.' I tell you, though he will not get up and give him the bread because he is his friend, yet because of the man's boldness he will get up and give him as much as he needs. "So I say to you: Ask and it will be given to you; seek and you will find; knock and the door will be opened to you. For everyone who asks receives; he who seeks finds; and to him who knocks, the door will be opened."*

13.

WAITING ON GOD

Wait for the Lord: be strong and
take heart and wait for the Lord.
—*Psalm 27:14*

Although I'd rather not think about the future, I had to prepare for my eventual disability. By January 2011, our house had been on the market for 220 days. At first, we managed to get a few showings, which was more than other sellers were getting in this market. Our strategy was to list it high and see if there were any nibbles. If we had listed it low and sold it right away, we would've kicked ourselves, wondering if we could've sold it for more. Besides, I was still ambulatory and we were in no hurry to move. We then lowered the price every month or so. By January, it was listed near our original purchase price—there was no chance of getting back the $37,000 in improvements we put into the house. We fully expected that whoever wanted the house would offer less, so the price would give us room to negotiate.

We purchased the house at the peak of the housing bubble in 2006. Fortunately, we rode the wave of housing prices on two prior homes and rolled over that equity into this purchase. Also, we made aggressive payments over the last few years with the hope of paying off the note before Sara started college, so we have enough equity to give us an adequate down payment on the new home—if we can sell it for a decent price.

It is a burden to keep the house within a few hours of perfection for a showing. It is hard enough for us to keep the house clutter-free, but to do so with a preschooler and a toddler in the house is nearly impossible.

The house shows well, but there is always an excuse: The backyard is too small. The house is across from a cemetery. Love the house, but it is number two on our list. But we only need one buyer, a buyer who loves character and craftsmanship like we do. All we needed was for somebody to look at the house and fall in love with it as we did. Kristin prayed specifically that the house would sell by Saturday. "By 3:00," I added, "if we are going to be specific."

Friday came around, and we still did not have a showing scheduled. I sent an e-mail to our real-estate agent: "Is there anything we can do to stimulate interest? Our prayer is to have the house sold by 3:00 p.m. on Saturday, but that will not be likely if we don't get a showing."

She replied, "It is good to see that your humor is razor-sharp in spite of all that is going on."

I wasn't joking. I expected God to send a buyer for this house.

Saturday came and went without a showing. I was disappointed. So was Kristin. And so was my mom, who had been staying with us for a couple weeks. She helped us get the house clean and keep it clean for the showing, which didn't come. My mom said that she had not been so disappointed since Foo, a Lhasa Apso stud she used to breed dogs, ate a litter of his puppies.

I am impatient. A source of tension in my relationship with Kristin is when I'm left waiting for her. I'd never thought of myself as a timely person. I routinely run a minute late. But compared to Kristin, I am fairly punctual.

Our different styles became abundantly clear when I picked up Kristin from her apartment to drive to the Upper Peninsula for our wedding weekend. She was supposed to have all of her stuff in her apartment packed in boxes and stored prior to leaving. But when I arrived, her room was in complete disarray and she was reading a book—she was overwhelmed by the mess and waiting for my help.

Since then, I learned to bite my tongue—although my face says more than my mouth ever could—after waiting in the car for her to come out of the house. On more than one occasion, when leaving for a long road trip and after waiting in the car for forty-five minutes with the kids, we drove a mile down the road, and then had to turn back for something we forgot.

I've been waiting so long for this house to sell. God, I have had a lot of practice waiting—thank You for that. Now, please. I am ready. Let this house sell.

I am not asking God for much, except for this request I plead with God to sell the house, and for my health.

This is the challenge of faith. Waiting. Waiting for our house to sell. Waiting for a cure. Waiting for a miracle. Waiting on God, wondering if He'll answer my prayers, trying to understand the parable of the persistent neighbor.

KRISTIN'S JOURNAL, FEBRUARY 2011: *Glimpses of Heaven*

Rebecca is further down the path of this journey that I am now only beginning. Her husband was diagnosed with ALS at age thirty-seven when they had a newborn son. Their son is ten now and her husband is still alive. I told her, "I am hoping that Todd's disease progresses as slowly, but I don't want to spend the next ten years grieving."

"You learn to compartmentalize it," she told me.

My counselor told me that when there is a death, it normally takes someone "a year to get over it and a year to get on with it." Dealing with a terminal disease is not so clean and neat. Initially, with the diagnosis, there was the loss of the dream of a future together, but there are also continual losses. Now, Todd needs help buttoning his pants and threading his belt through the belt loops. Every few weeks, Todd has more loss of function.

I want to be happy, healed, and whole again. But the grief that I am experiencing is not something one can get over, easily. I am stressed and on edge, and I cry more than I used to. But I worry less, surprisingly, as I realize that so much of life is out of my control. I also worship more deeply from the heart. My mind and emotions are more engaged; I am more empathetic when I hear about someone else's pain. So maybe a grieving life is a good life too. Living with an ache is not comfortable. It is not what I desire, and it is not what I would choose. It is hard, but it is not all bad.

Sometimes life on this earth is pretty good: Our health is good. Our finances are good. Our children are healthy. Our marriage is happy. We are in a right relationship with God. We experience the natural beauty of God's creation.

Maybe these gifts are little glimpses of Heaven. If we didn't have the bad stuff, maybe we wouldn't have the desire to leave earth for Heaven. But if we didn't have the good stuff, we wouldn't know to desire Heaven either. Maybe we are on this earth so we will appreciate Heaven more.

OUR PRAYER

God, we know we will have trouble here on this earth. We thank You that this is not our final destination.

JOHN 16:33b *"In this world you will have trouble. But take heart! I have overcome the world."*

14.

WANTING

And my God will meet all your
needs according to his glorious
riches in Christ Jesus.
—*Philippians 4:19*

I want a truck," I joked in response to Kristin's questions of what I wanted for my birthday or Christmas. One year, she obliged and bought me a red Honda Ridgeline. That was Sara's idea; from a young age she has been a master gift-giver. Kristin asked her when she was only two what they should get dad. "A truck," she said. Last Christmas, when Sara was four, Kristin asked her what they should get dad. "Cowboy boots," she said with certainty. I love my cowboy boots. The only problem with the truck is that it is only an inch long.

I'd never been quite serious about getting the truck; I was content waiting for a windfall, like a huge bonus, but other wants and needs always came first. Now that I'm sick, I find myself wanting the truck and other things even more. I feel my heart should be less focused on material things now that I know I have limited time, but instead my desire grows.

Long before I was sick, I've been conflicted about indulging myself. In 1997, when I had returned to Minneapolis, after spending ten months in Kalamazoo, Michigan, I took a job with another marketing research firm making fifty-percent more in salary, and my rent was cut in half. So when the repairs on my seven-year-old Mazda pickup truck started adding up, and the master cylinder was going, I bought a newer vehicle: a 1995 Ford Thunderbird, a car I thought was cool at the time until I realized that Thunderbirds were purchased mostly by older folks who wanted a sportier version of the Ford Crown Victoria. I returned to work and told my manager that I had purchased the car. "It's self-indulgent," I confessed. "I should have fixed the truck."

He laughed. "The car is well within your means. It is perfectly acceptable for somebody with your income to purchase a new car, and even more so, a used car."

Now that I've matured and married, I am less conflicted purchasing expensive items as long as we adhere to financial principles: keeping a three- to six-month emergency fund and carrying no debt other than our mortgage. For that reason, we saved for two years prior to purchasing a used mini-van.

My desire for stuff is fueled by seeing other people's stuff. I desire a new truck more when I park in the company parking lot, particularly among the BMWs and Mercedes-Benzes. When I return to my working-class home in northern Minnesota— even in my ten-year-old, two-wheel-drive Dodge Ram pickup truck with the rust-holes on the bottom of the doors—my envy is kept at bay.

But is this desire wrong, if kept in proper perspective? There were men of God, such as Abraham and Solomon, who had great wealth. Is it sinful and self-indulgent to want a Ford F-150 SuperCrew with a towing package and a nineteen-foot Bayliner with an inboard-outboard 4.3L MerCruiser Alpha V6? I don't want other people's stuff, not in a covetous way. I want my own stuff that I buy with money that I earn. I just need to weigh the value: my desire for each purchase against the financial sacrifice.

After the diagnosis, I was regretful that I hadn't yet taken the plunge to purchase things that I really wanted because there was another part of the value formula that I hadn't previously considered: more than weighing my desire against the financial sacrifice, I must also consider how long I'll be able to use it. Although I really wanted that truck and boat, I might not be able to drive in a year. Some people progress with this disease so fast that they're unable to drive within months.

Still high on my list was a full frame digital SLR camera. I justified the purchase of a Canon 5D as it would be much more important to capture cherished memories. The camera has amazing picture quality and can record high-definition video.

The only issue is that having stuff requires more stuff. My Canon 5D takes high-quality video, but, unfortunately, my six-year-old Compaq PC cannot keep up with the 300 MB files. Now it is not a matter of what I want. I really need a MacBook Pro 15.4-inch with a 2.0 GHz Intel quad-code i7 CPU, 8GB RAM, and a 500GB 7,200RPM hard drive.

Hollywood romanticizes death. Hearing of my terminal disease, folks have offered what they thought to be helpful advice: "You should see *The Bucket List*.[7] It's really good." I haven't seen it, nor do I want to. I don't want to be reminded of all that I can't do.

Most people with terminal diseases do not have the health or finances for a bucket list. My progression is slow enough and my finances are strong enough that I can do a few things on my bucket list, and I realize how blessed I am for that. But my primary concern is for my family. I want to use my limited time and finances honorably.

The top item on my bucket list will be to build a handicap-accessible house. As a man, I want to provide for my family. Before life gets really challenging, I want to see Kristin and the kids settled in our new home with family nearby.

KRISTIN'S JOURNAL, FEBRUARY 2011:
Joy in the Midst of Sorrow

"God doesn't give us what we want. He gives us what we need." This was the lesson Todd and I were scheduled to teach for children's church today. The lesson was timely considering we still haven't had a showing for the house.

In children's church, we talked with the kids about the difference between needs and wants.

"I need dinosaurs," four-year old Hunter said.

"Do you really?"

"Well, no."

"What do you need to live?" I asked the kids.

"Water, food, our bodies," five-year old Caleb said.

What about when your body is wasting away? Having a body is a need, isn't it? Or maybe our only real need is having God and His presence in our lives.

I had a dream in which God called to me and said, "Kristin, I have something better for Todd and something good for you and the kids." Heaven really is better. We grieve that Todd will miss out on Sara's and Isaac's graduations, weddings, and our grandchildren. It doesn't seem fair for the kids to grow up without their dad. But then I think, "Some people live through those events without joy. What good is that?" We are living with joy today, in the midst of sorrow.

OUR PRAYER

It is easy to hold on tightly to our spouses, children, lives, and stuff. With a terminal disease, there is no holding on. It changes our health, relationships, finances, and perspective. We are thankful that it does not change You, our God.

JAMES 1:17 *Every good and perfect gift is from above, coming down from the Father of the heavenly lights, who does not change like shifting shadows.*

15.

BEING USEFUL

In a large house there are articles not only
of gold and silver, but also of wood and clay;
some are for noble purposes and some for
ignoble. If a man cleanses himself from the
latter, he will be an instrument for noble
purposes, made holy, useful to the Master
and prepared to do any good work.
—*2 Timothy 2:20*

With ALS, the limits keep changing, and I find myself able to do less and less. A blizzard rolled in on Groundhog Day and shook the house all night long. We still had white-out conditions the next morning as I ate my breakfast and then initiated a conference call and live web-demo for an exciting project at work. By 10:30 a.m., the wind settled down and the sky turned blue. As I suited up in my snow bibs and jacket, I could see my neighbor had already cut a swath through the three-foot drifts on the north sidewalk of our corner lot. That was the light stuff; the wind had blown around the house, making drifts as high as five feet on the west side.

Kristin pushed the front door open. I squeezed out and waded through thigh-deep snow under the eave to the garage. Then I began a five-hour project to dig out with my little, single-stage snow thrower—a machine with fast-rotating rubber paddles designed to clear up to six inches of snow. I felt confident that I could still handle snow removal; my arms were weak, but I was compensating by using my torso and legs. My body pressed against the baler bar and I pushed hard with my legs. I was managing fine. I was blessed with the help of neighbors on either side who came with their big, two-stage snow throwers to move the massive snow-plow drift at the end of the driveway. (A two-stage snow thrower has an auger that pushes snow up into a propeller that then throws the snow many feet.)

I came into the house at 3:30 p.m. I ate a late lunch and took a nap. When I woke and tried to get off the couch, my legs started cramping in the worst way. I cannot even describe the pain. I screamed in agony. Kristin pressed, pushed and pulled on my legs, while praying, "God, please stop the cramping, stop the pain." I had a sense I would feel better once standing. I got to my feet and took ibuprofen, calcium, magnesium, and pantothenic acid. For a week thereafter, my legs were sore as if I ran a marathon.

It is difficult to adapt, especially for me, since I tend to test limits. When I was a boy, I climbed a young tree to the very top. I was holding on to the thin trunk next to me, swaying in the wind. The tree started to bend over, and, suddenly, I was holding on to the thin trunk above me. The branch snapped and I plunged to the ground. I paused every second or so to break another branch on my descent—snap, snap, snap, snap. Thump! I hit the ground. As I lay on my back, I looked up, through what should have been foliage, to a blue sky. My ribs bloodied and swollen, I was stunned, but I felt invincible, like a superhero who fell from a two story building and survived.

Wisdom has helped me avoid repeating the exact experiences; for years I would look up at the bare side of that tree and know not to attempt to climb the other side of it. For the rest of the winter, I looked at those piles of snow—which took nearly till spring to melt—and I knew I would not try to dig out from a blizzard again. I was humbled. I was not so tough after all. It became increasingly difficult to even shovel an inch of snow from the walks. I began to ask myself if I would be useful anymore.

My favorite tools are the ones most useful—my tile saw that does one thing really well, or my saws-all that does a lot of things pretty well. Val and John, my sister and brother-in-law, are useful like that, but even more so as they do a lot of things really well. When they visited in October to help out around the house, John tackled projects I hadn't the time or strength to do. He raked, mowed, trimmed hedges, and pulled flowers out of the window boxes. I asked if he would touch up the paint on the trim of a particular window. He touched up the trim around my entire house.

John asked if he could borrow my tile saw. I said, "Of course, take it. I won't be able to use it again."

That tile saw has been useful. I purchased it in 2001 when I remodeled my Milwaukee condo. From there, my Dad borrowed it to build a Habitat for Humanity house in Minnesota. Danny's dad, Cecil, borrowed it to put in a kitchen floor. I got it back to install my kitchen floor in my Racine house. It went back to Minnesota where John used it for his entry way, then to cut agates for a girl at church. My dad used it for his bathroom floor. I got it back again, with a new blade somewhere along the way, to install my patio.

I've been useful too. I looked after our old neighbor in Milwaukee as he was dying of cancer. I cleared the snow off the sidewalks for our Racine neighbors two down on each side—what I called my snow-blowing ministry, but really I just like to snow blow. I mowed our elderly neighbor's lawn. I've been helpful at work, willing to answer questions. *How can I be useful after this disease robs me of my strength and voice?*

My sister Valerie wished she could do more, but her back was hurting when she and John arrived, having slept a night on a bad hotel mattress. She made an appointment with Kristin's chiropractor and came home with a loaner walker and orders to stay off her feet. She apologized that she couldn't be more useful, but it was just a blessing to have her with us. And her bad back forced her to slow down, to spend less time folding laundry and more time bonding with Sara. Sara didn't care that Val couldn't move around much; she had the love and affirmation of her auntie.

I wonder about the future when I will spend most of my time sitting in a chair. As I wonder how I can continue to be useful, I look to others. In Houghton, Michigan, there is a college professor with ALS who is doing research on the genetics of the disease. Joel Cutler was a Canadian with ALS. He had a website about his thoughts and experiences.[8] He was an encouragement to other PALS and caregivers. He was useful. Another man with ALS, Andy, was, as his wife described, "a constant presence in his children's lives." Isn't that enough?

KRISTIN'S JOURNAL, FEBRUARY 2011: *Why Is God Allowing This?*

"God is in control."

"You are right where He wants you."

"God has a plan."

"He won't give you more than you can handle."

These statements, intended to comfort, sometimes seem hollow. Last fall, I asked my counselor if he thought it is true that God doesn't give us more than we can handle.

"I think that God always gives us more than we can handle," he said. "Life's unfair and unkind at times. The question is how do we muddle through?"

Since Todd's diagnosis, I have been struggling to comprehend why God is allowing this in our lives, and why there is so much suffering in the world. In John, Chapter 9, in the story of Jesus and the blind man, the disciples ask Jesus, "Who sinned, this man or his parents, that he was born blind?"

"Neither," Jesus replies, "But this happened so that the work of God might be displayed in his life."

Did God cause the man's blindness, or did it happen as part of living in a broken world? In Acts 10:38, disease is attributed to Satan. Does Satan cause disease? Did Satan cause Todd's ALS?

"Is God active in our suffering?" I asked my counselor. "Does He cause it? Or does He allow it as part of a fallen world?"

He shrugged. "Either way, God is ultimately responsible, isn't He?"

I can't wrap my mind around God's sovereignty paired with the bad things that happen in life. But maybe I don't need to. Maybe the point of the story of the blind man is that God, through His grace, can redeem any situation, and even bring out of it purpose and meaning.

"Do you think that God planned your ALS or

do you think He allowed it to happen?" I asked Todd.

"I don't know," he replied. "What I do know is that there is a right way to respond."

Maybe we don't need to have it all figured out; rather, we need to trust that God is in control and is working in our lives. God gives us more than we can handle, but it is not more than He can handle.

OUR PRAYER

God, we thank You that this world is not all there is. One day, You will make things right again.

REVELATION 21:1, 3-4 *Then I saw "a new heaven and a new earth," for the first heaven and the first earth had passed away. ... And I heard a loud voice from the throne saying, "Look! God's dwelling place is now among the people, and he will dwell with them. They will be his people, and God himself will be with them and be their God. He will wipe every tear from their eyes. There will be no more death or mourning or crying or pain, for the old order of things has passed away."*

16.

DREAMING

He has sent this message to us in Babylon:
It will be a long time. Therefore build
houses and settle down: plant gardens
and eat what they produce.
—*Jeremiah 29:28*

From the warmth of the old farm house, I looked across the snow-covered field and imagined sitting in the new house. Green fir trees surrounded the field, bejeweled with ice crystals from a wet snow followed by an overnight freeze. We were visiting Kristin's parents in the Upper Peninsula.

I'm looking forward to moving to the U.P. After we build the house, and if I'm still able to work, my company may allow me to work remotely. I work with people from across the world, and there is little need for me to be physically located in Racine. We rarely have meetings with people physically in the same conference room. With the use of communication tools, like Voice over Internet Protocol and desktop sharing, I can be effective from any location as long as I have a high-speed Internet connection.

Kristin, Lani, and the kids were in the kitchen eating breakfast. My father-in-law, David, and I were in the living room. "Sara was hoping to go sledding," I told David.

"Oh," he said, "I should build another sledding hill." The prior winter, he made a sledding hill with his plow truck. As David put on his jacket, he said, "I had the snowmobile tuned up. Come out with me and I'll drag it out with the truck. Maybe Sara wants to go for a ride."

I was more excited than Sara to ride on the snowmobile. My dad had a sled when I was a kid, so I would be re-living childhood memories. I took it for a spin around the house, and then around the field, without a helmet, but it was warm and I was driving at slow speeds. David sculpted the sledding hill with talent like a chainsaw artist carving bears out of logs.

An hour later, David had the sledding hill built. Sara came out of the house, we slid down the hill a few times, and then rode the snowmobile. We zipped around the field, and as we came toward the house, Kristin brought Isaac out. He was yelling, pointing at us on the snowmobile. He wanted to ride. Isaac was only one and a half, but he's my boy.

I parked the snowmobile at the base of the sledding hill. Sara jumped off, and Kristin placed Isaac in front of me. We went for a ride around the house, and then I stopped, wondering if he had enough of the cold wind in his face, but he demanded more. We went for a ride around the field; he demanded still more. A half hour later he had enough, but I hadn't. Kristin took Isaac and Sara into the house, and I stayed out to explore the field.

I rode to the location of the new house and drove up and down the future driveway. I parked the sled for a few minutes in the location of the future living room, and imagined the view. The prior July, I had laid a blanket to picnic with Sara there, on the grass by a grove of Fraser Firs that Kristin's family had planted nearly two decades ago. I asked Sara, "What should we call our new house?"

"The Christmas Tree House!" she said.

I went back around the field when I spied a mound that David had plowed a few hundred feet beyond his driveway. I drove to the mound and accelerated up to the top, then paused for a second. I gave the sled a little gas and rolled gently down the other side. *That was fun.* I took a couple more spins around the field, getting bolder and faster. I came around the house and raced toward the mound from the other direction. Again, I zipped up and paused at the top, and then I rolled gently down the other side into the deep snow. The sled stopped, nose down—the snow so heavy and wet that the skis got stuck—and in slow motion the momentum of my body carried me over the handlebars and off the front of the snowmobile. I landed on my face, buried in the wet snow, and my legs continued over my body as my neck bent back. Flop! My body landed in the snow and my head popped out.

I lay there dazed. *Is my neck broken? No. I am fine.* Good thing my neck was straight; I could've broken it and accelerated the whole process of becoming completely paralyzed. I imagined being rushed to the emergency room. The doctor would say, "Son, I'm so sorry, but you broke your neck. You will never walk again and you've lost the use of your arms."

"They were going, anyway," I would say.

We met our builder at the factory showroom located in Wisconsin, about halfway between Racine and the Upper Peninsula. We're using open panel construction, which means the walls and rafters would be built in a factory then assembled on site with a crane moving each section into place. We needed to select options—siding, shingles, etc.—and met with the designer on the layout of the house.

We had already designed the basic layout using consumer-grade software. The designer would turn those concepts into actual blueprints.

We designed 1,800 square feet with a great room concept. The garage and entrance are on the north side of the house. The living room, dining room, and kitchen are along the south-facing side, where we have several windows to gain passive solar heat in the long cold winters. There is a small room off the living room that will serve as a guest bedroom as we anticipate, when I need more care, my sister or mother staying with us for periods of time.

Using a design element from Frank Lloyd Wright, the vestibule has a lower ceiling making the space feel cramped, but as one steps into the great room the ceiling pops up another foot making the space feel large. We separate spaces throughout the house with different ceiling heights and flooring. We have tile on the kitchen and the dining room floors and hardwood in the living room. We have a bench seat on the east wall at the end of the living room, with a soffit above and shelving on each side of the bench. The house will be on one level, built on a cement slab with no basement.

We had met with a woman in Racine who built an addition for her husband who had ALS, and she was helpful in giving us tips for designing our own house. The hallway leading to the bedrooms is four feet wide and all of the doors are three feet wide to allow for accessibility in a wheelchair. The master bathroom is handicap-accessible with no lip to get into the shower. The toilet is set off two feet from the outside wall so that there is room for a person on each side to assist me.

We spent over an hour with the designer as we walked through each part of the house and discussed which aspects need to be accessible. The kitchen need not accommodate me. My arms were already weak, so I did not anticipate doing much of anything in the kitchen in the months or years ahead.

We explained to the designer that we were still concerned with the hallway and entrance into the master bedroom. "We don't like that the door into the bedroom requires a ninety-degree turn at the end of the hallway, but I'm not sure where else the door could go."

The designer asked if I'd be able to get into the kids' bedrooms.

"Probably not."

"Maybe I could put in a little cul-de-sac at the end of this hallway so that you will be able to turn your wheelchair around and get into each of the kids' bedrooms."

"That would be great."

We wrapped up with the designer, and then took a tour of the showroom picking out siding, shingles, countertops, and cabinets. Once everything was selected, we were on our way. The builder took a few weeks to price everything out and gave us a firm quote.

It was surreal planning for my eventual full disability and paralysis, but at the same time, it was fun because I was being creative, and rewarding because I was moving forward with life.

The often quoted verse, Jeremiah 29:11, could feel discouraging when one is facing a terminal disease. "'For I know the plans I have for you,' declares the Lord, 'plans to proper you and not to harm you, plans to give you hope and a future.'" I have a disease with no hope of a cure. I do not fear death, but my path to get there will not be pleasant. I have the hope of heaven, but what about life in the meantime?

Jeremiah writes that the people were going to be in captivity for 70 years. That's a long time to wait for release. Some would die in captivity. There is direction for what to do while waiting: Build houses and settle down. Plant gardens and eat what they produce. Keep living. Move forward with life as it is.[9]

I want to build my dream house in the U.P. and once we are in the country, we may even have a big garden.

KRISTIN'S JOURNAL, FEBRUARY 2011: *Action*

"Grief needs action to feel better, both emotional and physical." Christina Rasmussen wrote this quote on Second Firsts, an on-line grief community on Facebook of which I am part.

When some people face tragedy, they do something with it. Christina lost her thirty-five-year-old husband to terminal cancer when they had two small children. She was a grief counselor, but did not think she should be counseling when she herself was going through grief, so she took a job in human resources and went back to school. Christina rebuilt her life and then started a Facebook page, website, and a business called Second Firsts that encourages thousands of people who experience grief. She shares quotes and asks questions, and people share their own experiences.[10]

Christina's statement about "grief feeling better with action" resonated with me. Designing the handicap-accessible dream house was a project that re-energized us for living. Todd and I spent time looking through house design books for ideas. How could we add character to a small house without breaking the bank? We added a little nook for the desk and a window seat in the living room. We talked to a friend who had lost her husband to ALS. What design elements should we include to make the house handicap-accessible? We incorporated a roll-out patio and roll-in shower. We planned the rooms to maximize southern sun exposure in the living room and kitchen, while we minimized north-facing windows, to save on heating costs. Designing the house took creative energy and the collaboration of ideas. It gave us something to talk about other than ALS. It felt good to do something.

Joni Eareckson Tada, who was in a diving accident when she was seventeen and became a quadriplegic, has also done something with heartache in her life. I heard Joni speak at a conference when I was a college student. Everyone applauded her with a standing ovation after her talk from her wheelchair. Her message was moving because she has lived her faith in suffering. I have found comfort in reading several of her books this year. Joni has not become bitter over her years. Rather, she has become godly and has given hope to many through her ministry, Joni and Friends.

Joni and Friends puts on retreats for families dealing with disabilities. Their Wheels for the World program provides wheelchairs and the gospel message to those in the developing world. They provide education and training in disability ministry. Joni has written many books that encourage people in their faith, especially those who face suffering and disability. As Joni currently deals with chronic pain, she says her ministry to people affected by disability is why she gets out of the bed in the morning.[11]

When Christina and Joni faced hardship, they found a new sense of purpose in helping others. I also want to do something with pain. I want to find meaning and make our suffering count for something, even if just by valuing relationships more, enjoying the time we have, and finding beauty in the small things.

OUR PRAYER

God, as we face disease, we keep living.
Give us courage and strength as we
take action and make new plans.

JOSHUA 1:9 *Have I not commanded you? Be*
strong and courageous. Do not be terrified;
do not be discouraged, for the Lord your
God will be with you wherever you go.

17.

SHARING OUR SITUATION

My mouth will speak in praise of the Lord.
—Psalm 145:21a

We used to get the local newspaper delivered to our door every morning. Sara insisted on getting it from the front porch. Kristin took the paper out of the thin plastic bag, opened up the bag, scooped it full of air, and then twisted the top closed making a balloon. Sara popped the bag, delighting her each and every time. But that was not reason enough to subscribe to the paper. We enjoyed reading it, but Kristin canceled our subscription last summer after the diagnosis when we were too focused on our own situation to worry about the problems in our city and world.

Nonetheless, on a Monday in early March, a newspaper happened to show up, unsolicited, on our door step. "Yea! We got a paper today," Kristin exclaimed.

"Can I pop the bag?" Sara asked.

Kristin sat and read the paper with her quinoa and raisins. I slipped two pieces of gluten-free bread into the toaster.

"Hey, Rob is in the paper. He won a fishing trip with his dad and sons." Kristin told me of a man who had been in a small group Bible study with us a few years ago.

"Good for him."

I drank the carrot juice that Kristin made for me and swallowed my breakfast pills. I put my lunch pills in a baggie. My toast popped and I spread almond butter and jam on both pieces. I kissed my family goodbye, telling each of them, "God loves you, I love you, have a good day," and I headed out the door for work, a short ten-minute drive.

As I arrived in the parking lot, my cell phone rang—Kristin calling.

"You need to write a plan about your dream to build the Christmas Tree House. We could win $100,000. Check your e-mail; I sent you a link."

"What are you talking about?"

"The Dockers contest. Rob won $2,000 for the weekly Man Grant. But they have a $100k grand prize in the Wear the Pants contest. You've got to make it good."

Up in my office, the first thing I did was check my e-mail. There was a message from Kristin about the Dockers contest. I clicked on the link that directed me to the company's Facebook page. *A Facebook contest, stink. I'll need to sign up for Facebook.* I had resisted becoming part of the social network for years, rather proudly. Nonetheless, I signed up, and then turned my attention to the essay.

The Dockers page said, "Get Scrappy. Get your friends to vote for your plan." I needed to write 400 characters on what I would do with $100,000 to make my dream come true.

After ten minutes, I came up with this: "The doctor said, 'You have ALS.' It was June 11, 2010. I've been losing strength with this terminal disease. It's been my dream to live in the Upper

Peninsula of Michigan. Now more than a dream, we want to be near family for my wife and two small kids. We selected a builder and designed a handicap-accessible home. We need to sell our house, but we've had few showings. The clock is ticking."

Three hundred ninety-two characters; I am not sure what else to say. I entered the contest and submitted the plan along with a few pictures. I was contestant 29,421. It appeared the numbers were assigned sequentially, so winning would be a long shot.

There were three rounds to the contest. In round one, people on Facebook voted for a plan. The top fifty vote-getters advanced to round two, during which the company selected five finalists. In round three, people on Facebook again voted for their favorite of the five.

The unfortunate part for me was that I was a month late to the contest. There was only a week left of voting. But when I browsed through several other plans, I found that most had less than 100 votes. In fact, I only came across one other with more, and he only had 342.

I clicked back to the Facebook page a few times throughout the day and saw the number of votes climbing up—thirty-four, forty-eight, sixty-three, etc.

"Kristin, do you see the votes? Who's voting for us?"

"I'm working it on Facebook, sending notes to my friends. What would you think of being interviewed by the paper?"

"For real?"

"Yeah, Amanda knows a reporter at the local paper and said that she would tell her about us and maybe she would do a story. I posted on my wall asking if anybody has ideas of how to drum up support on the Internet for a cause like ours. Amanda responded with the idea to get a story in the paper."

Amanda is a woman Kristin knows from a local mom's group. She is a go-getter, the type of person you want working for you. She once advocated for changes to a city ordinance against raising chickens. She hoped to keep a few hens so her kids could collect eggs and see where food came from. The newspaper ran an article about her efforts, so she knew a few reporters.

"Sure, let's give it a try," I replied. "Even if this contest doesn't go anywhere, it will raise awareness for ALS. In all things God works for the good of those who love Him."

Later that night, I said, "I think we will break 100 tonight. This is crazy."

On Tuesday, the vote count kept climbing. Kristin became a master of social networking. She posted links on her Facebook account. She sent messages to Facebook friends. She sent messages to old friends with whom she had lost contact.

The outpouring of support was encouraging. Some friends and family who were not on Facebook signed up just to vote. Even Kristin's brother, who is usually laid back, contacted his hometown paper with a letter to the editor. The word spread to old friends, who hadn't yet heard the news of my diagnosis, and they sent sympathetic notes and, of course, they said they would vote every day.

Late Tuesday morning, Kristin called me at work. "The reporter e-mailed me, and asked if we were interested in sharing our story. She has time later this afternoon to interview us."

"Sure, even if this contest doesn't go anywhere, the article would be worth it if we could bless just one person."

The reporter and a photographer came to our house. The reporter talked with us for over two hours. We shared our story: how I first noticed that my left arm wasn't working and the diagnosis; how we processed it; how our faith helped us cope; and how we hoped to win the contest.

She said that she would write the story that night, and that it would come out on either Thursday or Friday.

By the end of Tuesday, we picked up a couple hundred more votes. We broke 300 before going to bed.

Over the next week, the vote went up exponentially each day. The newspaper story ran on Friday, and the vote count exploded after that. It seemed to go viral. People from across the country and even people in Europe and Brazil were voting for me and posting encouraging messages.

One week later, we ended with 3,412 votes, which was, from what we could tell, the second highest. We received notification that we made it in the top fifty. Even so, I still believed it was a long shot. I reviewed Dockers' market and brand, tapping into my knowledge base from my early career in marketing research. The target market is twenty-five- to forty-year-old men who wear business casual to work and want to look thinner. Said another way, the pants are worn by pudgy professionals—that's me. But their image is that of hip, urban, thin men in alternative jobs. I told Kristin, "They will probably pick five guys who better fit their image."

Dockers kept us waiting for weeks. The day before the five finalists would be announced for the final round of voting, I received a rejection e-mail.

"I know it was a long shot, but I am so disappointed," Kristin told me in tears.

"It is like buying a lottery ticket, and then being crushed when you don't win the jackpot," I told her. "I have been through enough job interviews, thinking I had nailed the interview, only to get a rejection—and that was when I was only one of two or three candidates. Being rejected from a group of fifty is hardly worth a sigh."

However, some good came out of the contest. For one thing,

it got me on Facebook. One can argue if that is good, but Facebook is a useful tool to reconnect with old friends and to reach out to new ones. We got encouragement from people, and maybe the article was an encouragement to others who were facing similar difficulties. I'd do it again in a heartbeat.

The next day, I logged on to Facebook to see who Dockers picked—five young skinny guys with alternative business ideas: furniture restoration, a microbrewery, environmental education, a fiction magazine, and clay baked bread. The college student who wanted to provide environmental education won the $100k prize. I won the *grand* prize—the love and support of the community.

KRISTIN'S JOURNAL, MARCH 2011:
Prayers for Healing

"What might happen if we make our story public?" I speculated to Jana. "Hopefully, someone will see the article and want to buy our house. Maybe someone will show up wanting to pray for us or someone will show up with alternative therapy ideas, but I am not opposed to those anyway."

The day after the article ran, I received a call from a guy who told me he was a health coach in New York. He claimed that ALS was curable. I told him that I was Todd's health coach and I gave Todd a lot of supplements, juiced vegetables every morning and gave him a nightly massage. I was open to new ideas, if he had any to offer, but I requested references from people he had cured. He was not forthcoming, and he got the message that I was not going to be taken for a ride.

We also got a call from a local guy named Jesse, who said he was moved with compassion when he read our story. He wanted to pray for us. I asked him where he went to church; I wanted to be sure he wasn't in a cult. He said he sometimes went to a church with which I was familiar, but he attended a lot of different churches. He was happy to pray over the phone with us or meet us in person. I thought it was a nice offer, a little unusual, but nice. I said I would talk to Todd and get back to him.

I called my mom and told her about the conversation and proposed meeting. "Sometimes people on the fringe have a closer walk with God," she said excitedly.

I ran the idea by my brother. "He probably doesn't go to one church because he doesn't fit in anyone's box," he observed.

Todd was uninterested, at first, saying, "Tell him he can pray for us from his home. That's biblical. Jesus healed the man's daughter from a distance because of the man's faith."

"Sometimes, it is a blessing for people, though, to let them be a blessing," I said. We decided to see if Jesse wanted to meet us at our church after the service, and he agreed.

Todd and I knew who he was when we saw him sitting a few pews in front of us: a casually dressed young guy in his twenties whom we didn't recognize. "That's got to be him," Todd said. "He is worshiping with more enthusiasm than a typical visitor."

After the service, we found him in the lobby, waiting expectantly with a big smile on his face. We went to the infant nursery, which was by then empty, and pulled a few chairs together.

Jesse talked about Christ's compassion. "When Jesus saw the crowds He had compassion on them. He healed people because of His compassion." Jesse read Isaiah 53:5, "But he was pierced for our transgressions, he was crushed for our iniquities; the punishment that brought us peace was upon him, and by his wounds we are healed." Jesse told us he believes that God does not want us to suffer and that He wants to physically heal us.

Jesse asked if he could lay hands on Todd while he prayed for him.

Todd hesitated, and I asked Jesse, "Have you heard of Joni Eareckson Tada? After Joni was in a diving accident and became a quadriplegic, a lot of people prayed for her healing. When people accused her of not having enough faith to be healed, she would turn it around and tell them to read the story of the paralyzed man: Scripture says that Jesus healed the paralyzed man because of his friends' faith. Scripture doesn't mention the paralyzed man's faith at all." I wanted to get a sense of whether or not Jesse's prayer was going to accuse us of lacking faith.[12] "We pray persistently every night that God would heal Todd and we welcome similar prayers," I told Jesse. "Sometimes Christians aren't healed though."

Todd pointed out, "Everyone except Enoch and Elijah, who were taken up, eventually dies."

Jesse reassured us that it was not his intent to judge our faith. Jesse and I laid our hands on Todd's shoulders, and Jesse prayed for healing; he prayed specifically for Todd's nerves; and he prayed that we would be encouraged.

We do not know if God will heal Todd, but it was encouraging to be prayed over by someone who truly believed God could and would heal Todd.

OUR PRAYER

God, You use Your church, people with many different gifts, to encourage and strengthen us. You are a big God.

1 CORINTHIANS 12:4-6 *There are different kinds of gifts, but the same Spirit. There are different kinds of service, but the same Lord. There are different kinds of working, but the same God works all of them in all men.*

18.

ACCEPTING HELP

Help the weak, remembering the words
the Lord Jesus himself said: 'it is more
blessed to give than to receive.'
—*Acts 20:35b*

The difference between a disability and an un-ability is the expectation of ability. I have happy kids, although they are unable do many things for themselves. They're clothed and sheltered. When they are hungry, we cook for them. They do not have yet an expectation for independence; they just trust that we will be there to help them. I have a disability because there is an expectation that a forty-year-old man should be able to do more. As my independence decreases, I'm happy knowing there are people around to help me—friends, family, and even strangers.

Settled in my new position as the manager of diagnostics and monitoring on the global manufacturing team, I was asked in January to attend a March meeting in Argentina with the regional directors. I was to go on the trip as I was leading a key project to establish a process to collect and report key performance indicators for all of the company's factories around the world.

In making the flight arrangements for the business trip, I mirrored my director's itinerary—same shuttle to the airport and same flights. Raul lived close to my house, so it would be convenient. I mentioned to Raul that I would be on the same flight as he, and asked if he would mind helping me. By that point, I was not keeping my diagnosis a secret, but I hadn't told Raul about it because I no longer needed much time off for doctors' appointments. He didn't seem at all perplexed that I would ask, so I suspected he knew.

"Did you know that I was sick?"

"Yes, yes, I did," he said. "I'm so sorry to hear that." He asked me questions about the disease and said, looking down in reflection, that it had caused him to think much about his life and priorities.

Our real-estate agent had scheduled an open house for Sunday, so we needed to get the house ready. Kristin and the kids were going to her parents' home for the week, leaving on Sunday morning, and the shuttle driver was to pick me up from the house at 1:45 p.m. for the drive to the airport.

After the news of my diagnosis became public, when the local paper ran the article about the diagnosis and my dream to build a handicap-accessible home in the Upper Peninsula of Michigan, the word spread around my company. A few of my colleagues reached out to me and offered to help with whatever we needed.

So a few days prior to the Argentina trip, I sent an e-mail to them asking if anyone was available to help clean the house on Saturday morning. Ali was free and more than willing to come over. We turned her loose on a pile of unfolded laundry. I was a bit embarrassed that my co-worker was folding my underwear, and it must have entered Kristin's mind too, as Kristin commented that she was glad I threw out my ratty, holey, worn briefs.

The house was clean by Saturday afternoon, but living with a five-year-old and a toddler, the house stays clean for only so long.

On Sunday morning, we still had quite a mess ahead of us before we could leave the house. It seemed that as much as we cleaned, there was an equal size mess left in Isaac's wake. I tried to convince Kristin to go. Kristin wanted to take care of as many of the repetitive and heavy tasks as she could, but I was getting exhausted chasing Isaac around, perhaps as much as if I had been cleaning myself. I said, "I love you, but you have to go. I've got this."

Kristin left at 10:00 a.m. I kept working on the house until 1:00 p.m. I had forty-five minutes to relax, and I did so in a clean house.

There were two legs of the flight to Argentina: a three-hour flight from Chicago to Miami and a nine-and-a-half-hour overnight flight from Miami to Buenos Aires. My company allows us to purchase business-class tickets for international flights. They also have a business-to-coach rebate program, whereby if I purchase a coach ticket, my company will rebate to me a few hundred dollars in cash per leg. After the quote for building our dream house came in about $40,000 more than I wanted to see, I felt like I needed all the cash I could get, so I ordered a cheap ticket. *A night sitting in a coach seat wouldn't kill me.*

At the airport, Raul was incredibly helpful. It was difficult for me to lift a bag—not due to lack of strength, but due to lack of opportunity. Raul grabbed my bags as if he were a bellman.

I worked at a four-star hotel in Minneapolis during college. The rumor was that the Moroccan bellman was the highest-paid employee at the hotel, clearing over $80,000 in salary and tips, mostly tips. He made his tips not only by carrying bags well, but by remembering names—plus every detail ever spoken to him—of the loyal guests. Raul is not a bellman, rather a director at a multi-national company. He has achieved much success in his career, not just by doing management well, which he does, but, like the Moroccan bellman, by being so personable while doing it.

I got in line behind an older couple when the airline announced pre-boarding for those who needed special assistance. I told the gate agent that I needed to board early due to a disability. He asked if I needed a chair. I said, "No, but I will need help with my bags." He told me to continue down the jet bridge and that somebody would help on the plane. Once on the plane, I was embarrassed, being a young man of forty years asking a fifty-something, short, heavy, gray-haired flight attendant to lift my bags. She didn't think twice.

The flight from O'Hare to Miami was difficult. My muscles became stiff and started cramping. I was noticeably limping as I walked off the plane. My calf muscles had locked up to the point where I felt like I was wearing two casts.

We had a two-hour layover in Miami, which was extended to three, with an hour delay. My flight to Argentina was scheduled to leave at midnight. Raul was on a mission to get an upgrade to business class. He also took advantage of the business-to-coach rebate program, perhaps because he wanted the cash, but, more so, because he had so many frequent flyer points that he could get the cash and a business-class seat with a free upgrade.

Two other directors were on the same flight. Raul and I met up with them in the Admirals Club, to which Raul had access because he was a frequent flyer, and to which I had access because

I was Raul's guest. The four of us sat at a high, round table and ordered drinks and dinner.

My dinner—a salad with turkey, pear and gorgonzola—arrived at the table and I took a few bites. Then they announced that our flight was boarding, so I shoveled the last of my salad down my throat. On the way out, Raul stopped to talk to the agent at the Admirals Club desk again about getting an upgrade. He kept trying long past the point that I would've given up. Raul waved me on, "I'll meet you at the gate." He turned back to plead with the agent.

I shuffled to the gate, my legs still stiff, either from the heavy cleaning that morning or from the flight from O'Hare, but probably from both, one after the other—exertion followed by the lack of movement. I walked so slowly that Raul, who was several minutes delayed, caught up to me as I approached the gate and urged me to step into the priority line as he passed me.

Once we reached the front of the line, he asked a gate agent, yet again, if he had an upgrade. The lady said, "You have to wait over here for a few more minutes."

Raul told me to go on, and yelled to me as I walked down the jet bridge, "Todd, the upgrade is for you if I get it. I'll come find you."

I didn't know what to say. I felt a lump in my throat.

When I got to my seat, a woman speaking broken English asked if I could help lift her bag into the overhead. I said, "Sorry, I cannot even lift my own bag." It must have seemed strange to her; I looked healthy. I waited there for a minute wondering how I would get my bags into the overhead myself. A young guy, perhaps my age, arrived at his seat in front of me. I asked him if he could help with my bags, and the lady's bags too. He was happy to help.

No sooner did I sit in my seat than Raul came down the aisle and said, "I got it. Which are your bags? I will get them."

Raul pulled my bags down from the overhead compartment. We crossed to the other aisle of the Boeing 777 and worked our way against the flow of people up to seat 10E.

Business class seats are amazing on international flights as they can recline to a near horizontal position. I fell asleep as soon as the plane reached altitude, and I woke up an hour from Buenos Aires.

Raul is my hero.

I am forced to be humble, receiving help when I am weak and unable to return the favor. Those who help me are fulfilling the Apostle Paul's admonishment to "help the weak," and they are blessed. I am blessed to receive their help, but I would still rather have the blessings of giving. I'll have to find new ways to give.

KRISTIN'S JOURNAL, MARCH 2011:
Coming to Grips with Life

As Todd headed off to Argentina, I drove with the kids to visit my parents for a week—the first road trip that I had taken with two kids by myself. It went well. After an hour and a half, we stopped at Subway for an early lunch. I was proud of my kids when they each ate a healthy lunch—salad with chicken on top. Then we got back on the road.

It was not as easy as traveling with Todd when I could get videos started and pass back books and snacks, but I managed to do a little of that while driving with one hand and keeping my eyes on the road. I felt competent. I was handling life.

Then I felt sad, missing Todd, not just missing him in Argentina, but thinking, "This is how it will be when I am a single mom." There is not the same joy as there is on a road trip with Todd. I enjoy chatting and spending quality time with him.

Before he left for Argentina, as I gave Todd a massage, he apologized to me, saying this was not what he had in mind for me when we got married. He wanted to provide for me, not have me become his caregiver. I told him not to think like that. It was not something he chose. Now if he had done something wrong, if he had had an affair, then I would be mad and he should apologize. But to apologize for ALS? I don't resent him. I am glad he has me. If I was going to be upset with anyone, it would be God. And I was, but not so much anymore.

I still don't understand why Todd has ALS, but I am starting to think more like Lou Gehrig, a Hall of Fame baseball player with the Yankees from 1923-39, who had ALS. In his famous speech on July 4, 1939, Gehrig called himself "the luckiest man on the face of the Earth." He chose to be thankful for his many opportunities.

I thank God for my blessings. I am thankful for my husband and best friend. We joke that while Todd is with us, at least he will retain his ability to listen to me talk. I am blessed to have Sara and Isaac. I am thankful for our supportive extended family, church, and our friends.

I am thankful for the company benefits Todd has. I am thankful that I have skills and wherewithal to navigate through resolving billing disputes with our insurance company. We have a lot for which to be thankful.

We arrived at my parents' house at bedtime. I put Isaac right into his crib and then tucked Sara into bed, between the Strawberry Shortcake sheets I used to sleep in. The kids are looking forward to riding in Papa's backhoe. I am thankful to have my parents' help for the week. I still ache for my kids and I am sad, but I am thankful that God is providing for our needs. We are going to be okay.

OUR PRAYER

God, You promise us Your peace when we present our requests to You with thanksgiving. We have prayed and petitioned. Now we say "thank You." Thank You for providing for our needs. Thank You for the people You have given us who help us.

PHILIPPIANS 4:6–7 *Do not be anxious about anything, but in everything, by prayer and petition, with thanksgiving, present your requests to God. And the peace of God, which transcends all understanding, will guard your hearts and your minds in Christ Jesus.*

19.

SAYING TOO MUCH

There is a time for everything, and a season for every activity under heaven. A time to be silent and a time to speak.
—*Ecclesiastes 3:1 & 7b*

Kristin was worried about me going to Argentina because I wouldn't have the massages she gives me to relax my muscles. We discovered the benefit of massage even before the diagnosis, as it was one thing we tried back when only my left arm was weak and I didn't know what the future held. After the diagnosis, the massages were focused on my arms, but over time I found that I was walking more stiffly, so Kristin worked on my legs too. She gave me massages every night, and if we missed a night, I noticed. I agreed that I would get massages at the hotel spa. Most hotels that cater to international guests have such services.

The plane ride, or the preparation before leaving, took a toll on my muscles. As I arrived on Monday morning, I was stiff—my calves especially. I walked as if I had casts on both legs, taking short, waddling steps. I made an appointment to have a massage that evening and another appointment for Wednesday.

Monday evening, the rest of the group went out for dinner and I returned to the hotel for my massage. Anticipating that the massage therapist might not speak English, I asked the spa receptionist to pass on instructions, "I need a deep, therapeutic massage focusing on my arms and legs. I don't need a back massage, and I don't need a relaxing Swedish massage." I told the receptionist that I have a medical condition that causes stiff muscles, and I needed the massage to relax my muscles.

I walked through the men's locker room and waited in a room with *chaises longues* and a basket of fruit. I waited less than a minute, and then a woman called from an opening door, "Todd," in a thick accent. She was thirty-something, short, rotund, and dark-skinned. We said our greetings, awkwardly as I speak little Spanish. All of the Spanish I know, I learned from Dora de Exploradora. Sara is a big fan. We tried to expose Sara to Spanish at a young age. Although we didn't believe that she would become fluent, we felt that her exposure to the language would train her ear to hear certain sounds. Later in life, it would come much easier for her to learn the language. I didn't take a foreign language until I was in college, and then only a couple years of German. My brain is not wired to think in a foreign language. I love language, I love learning words from various languages, but when it comes to conjugating sentences, I feel helpless. Nonetheless, I communicated well enough with the masseuse, and the massage was greatly beneficial.

During the meetings that week, I got out of my chair often to walk around and stretch. Standing close to the wall, I placed the ball of my foot on the trim with my heel on the floor, and, with my knee straight, I leaned toward the wall.

By Wednesday my muscles were feeling better, but they were still pretty stiff. On my way into the second massage, I realized I had forgotten to give the receptionist clear instructions on what I needed. As before, I walked through the men's locker room and waited on a *chaise longue*. This time, a European-looking lady, slender and about forty-five called my name, "Todd?" in what seemed like perfect English and no detectable Spanish accent. I was relieved; *I will be able to tell her my need for therapeutic massage.*

"Oh good, you speak English."

"No. Only a few words," she said, again without an accent.

This is hard to believe. Perhaps she, like Sara, was exposed to American English at a young age so that her ears were trained, and now her tongue could produce the words without an accent. But sure enough, she knew few English words. The lexicon of *Dora de Exploradora* would only take me so far; there were no episodes on the topic of deep, therapeutic massage.

I used simple words and pantomimes to express my need, but without her having heard the basic instructions, it was difficult for her to understand me. I tried to say that my muscles were sick, "Músculos," and I coughed and made a dreadful facial expression.

She filled in, "Enfermedad?"

"Si, enfermedad de la muscular," I said, pleased that we had reached an understanding on this complex topic.

"Ahh," she said, and began kneading harder.

"Si," I said in affirmation.

As before, we managed small talk. She complimented me on all of the Spanish words I knew; I used most all of them in that conversation. I credited Dora de Exploradora, and she laughed. I managed to tell her that I had a daughter and a son, "Hija cinco, y un hijo un años." She had one daughter who flew; she flapped her hands like bird wings. "Pilot?" I asked.

"No."

"Flight attendant?"

"Si."

At the end of the massage, I stood and thanked her. She said, again with little accent, "Your arms are bad." Her facial expression showed grave concern. "Your legs, okay, but tight. This is not good. Your arms, very bad."

Her empathy for me made me want to cry. It is so hard to explain this disease, even to those who share my language. *How can I explain to her?*

"I have terminal enfermedad de la muscular. Ah-Ellay-Essay. Do you know A-L-S?"

"No. Sorry. My English is no good."

"I have tres - cinco años …viva, then I will die." I motioned with my hand across my throat.

"No! No!" she gasped.

I don't know why I told her. Did she need to know? I was moved by her empathy for me, and wanted her to understand. Early in this disease, Kristin and I made a decision to be open. But does a certain amount of openness become intrusive? People have lives; they have enough to deal with. Do they really need to know?

I said too much. I reassured her, "It's okay, it's okay. El Señor es bueno. Mi casa está en cielos." I pointed toward Heaven.

"Yes," she said, replying in English, "But your home is here too."

We hugged and I slipped her a tip.

I didn't tell a lot of people of the diagnosis for the first three months. I wasn't ready to accept it myself, and I thought of the potential embarrassment of telling somebody that I had a terminal disease with no treatment, then later finding out it was a benign neuropathy. I've heard stories of PALS who've gone a year or longer without telling anybody of their diagnosis. I respect their decision, and realize they may have a motive that I haven't considered. But after I accepted the diagnosis, I found a catharsis in being open about the disease; it helped me through the grieving process.

Did people feel sorry for me? Perhaps, but what is wrong with people feeling sorrow for my suffering and distress? What's wrong with empathy when people understand and are sensitive to my experience? What's wrong with our society that we feel like we have to be perfect, healthy, faultless, and pain-free—or, at least, feel we have to act this way?

On the other hand, I don't want ALS to be salient in my conversations with others that it crowds out my ability to listen to them and understand their concerns. Life goes on; I can't stop living my life. I need to work, and while I am at work, I need to focus on my job. I need to spend time with Kristin and the kids, giving them my undivided attention. If I thought about ALS 24/7, I'd go nuts.

KRISTIN'S JOURNAL, MARCH 2011: *Compartmentalizing*

I am glad when people ask me how Todd is doing. Maybe some people don't ask because they think I don't want to talk about it, as if my life would be normal if they didn't bring it up. But I am always thinking of it now; that's my new normal.

Even a dead fish is viewed through the lens of ALS. Last fall, when I found Sara's betta fish, Gabby, lifeless at the bottom of the fishbowl, Todd suggested not telling Sara and getting another fish. But the ALS material I read suggested getting kids a fish so they have a concept of death before a parent dies. I am not a big fan of cleaning out the fishbowl every week and I have a lot going on, so I was not going to miss the fish. When Sara came for breakfast, I told her that something sad had happened—Gabby died. She burst into tears. I held my little girl and I cried too. I don't like to see her hurting. Then, reluctantly, I told her we could get another fish and she was happy. It's easy to replace a fish. Maybe I shouldn't have been so quick to replace Gabby. Maybe it would have been better preparation for Sara if I hadn't.

I talked to a friend on the phone yesterday. She and her husband have a son who is a little younger than Sara. They want more children, but haven't been able to have another one. Now, they are in the process of adopting a little boy from China. They hadn't originally planned on adopting. She had thought they would have another child, whenever God sent one. But now the biological clock is ticking; her husband is forty-three and she is thirty-six. They are starting to do the math, asking how old they will be when their kids graduate from high school. "We hadn't thought about the age factor before," she told me.

"Todd thought about it," I automatically replied. "He didn't want to be a really old dad when our kids graduated." I paused as I saw the bitter irony of what I was saying. I empathized with her situation using my old normal. I caught myself, "Well, you don't know what is going to happen in life. We make plans, but things don't always turn out the way we plan." I thought of the plaque on our windowsill that says, "A man's mind plans his way but the Lord directs his steps. Proverbs 16:9."

After I hung up the phone, I felt sad thinking about our future, but I was encouraged that I had compartmentalized it; that I had, for a minute, stepped out of my new normal and that the conversation did not bring me to tears.

OUR PRAYER

God, we make plans, but You are the one who controls our future. We thank You that our home is in Heaven. Without that hope, we could not face these difficult circumstances.

JOHN 14:1-2 *Do not let your hearts be troubled. Trust in God; trust also in me. In my Father's house are many rooms; if it were not so, I would have told you. I am going there to prepare a place for you.*

20.

ANSWERING QUESTIONS

When I was a child, I talked like a child,
I thought like a child, I reasoned like a child.
—*1 Corinthians 13:10a*

We had what seemed like a week of vacation in April, though I went to work every day, because Valerie and John used their vacation to come and help us. I have been humbled by the support that we've received over the last year. So many people have come beside us to help carry the heavy burden of life when everything in life has become heavy for me.

We did not need to tell my sister Val what to do. At the same time, she was respectful of our space and the way that we did things. She asked how we liked the towels folded, but it was not a question if she should fold them. And she cared for us so deeply, revealing that she hadn't been able to sit through a Sunday worship service without crying until recently—nearly ten months after the diagnosis. It only took me a few services.

John is not only my brother-in-law, but my brother-in-love. John hurts for me. I can see it in his eyes and I can feel it in his touch when he gently grabs my shoulder. It would be difficult to list all of the projects that John completed for me, replacing the front sidewalk being the biggest of them. What I most enjoyed was watching him lift Isaac above his head and fly him around like an airplane. Every boy needs to be flown around like an airplane.

Val tucked Sara into bed on several nights. Val told us one Saturday evening after tucking her into bed that Sara had questions about ALS. She said, "I told her, 'Well, you know that daddy's arms are getting weak, right?' Sara told me, 'Yes, but I know there's something else.'"

Valerie respectfully left the tough questions for us to answer.

We struggle with what to tell Sara, and someday Isaac. The advice that we have been given is to focus on the now. Kids don't have the same concept of time as do adults. There's little sense talking about life expectancy when Sara's weeks and months blur together and when she can hardly figure out the time of day—"Is this lunch or dinner?"

Sunday morning, after Val and John left, I sat at the table next to Sara while she was eating her oatmeal. I asked, "Sara, do you have any questions about ALS?"

"Yes, what is it?"

"You know when you are sick and your body wants to throw up? My body is sick, but instead of me wanting to throw up, my arms are getting weak. My arms will continue to get weak and so will my legs. Eventually, I'll need more help, like with putting on my socks," I said as I put on my socks getting ready for church. "Does that make sense?"

"Yes."

"Do you have any other questions?"

"What else is going on?" Sara asked.

"That's all, Sara. I'm sick. My muscles are getting weak and we want to move to the U.P. so that Neenee and Papa can help us."

"I am not sure if Papa actually told me that he will build a swing set for me," she told me somberly with her head down.

"I am sure he would be happy to."

"Do you build it or buy it?" Sara asked.

"Both. You buy it, and then you have to assemble it. Do you have any other questions?" I asked as Sara, still with her head down, was fiddling underneath the table.

"Yes, why do I keep putting my pinkies in the holes under the 'tabled?'" She looked up and smirked.

I'm not a car guy, but I gawked at a Honda Element that pulled into a handicap-accessible space in a store parking lot. Something was different about it. I was waiting in the van with the kids, backed into the parking space, keeping an eye on the entrance of the store for Kristin to come out. The SUV was in my line of sight. The driver-side doors opened, both front and rear doors, in a smooth, mechanical motion—automatic doors, opening like French doors with the rear door hinged on the rear-side. A ramp came down off the driver's door and a man rolled out. I watched him wheel into the store.

The guy in the wheelchair managed to get in and out of the store before Kristin had come out. I stepped out of the van and waved to the guy as he was approaching his vehicle. I asked if he'd mind talking to me for a few minutes over by my van so I could keep an eye on the kids. I asked about his SUV—where he found it and how much it cost to convert it. I told him that I was curious because someday I might need to make a similar purchase. We talked about my condition and about his accident. He gave me his telephone number in case I had any other questions, and then he left.

When Kristin got back into the van, I told her about the SUV and said, "He lost the use of his legs in a snowmobiling accident."

"Daddy," Sara asked, "are you going to lose your arms?"

"Well, I won't lose my arms..." I hesitated.

Kristin jumped in, "Daddy won't lose his arms, but the doctors don't have any medicine to make them better, so his arms will keep getting weaker and his legs will get weak too. He might need a wheelchair, and that is why he was interested in that man's car."

Most advice for telling little kids about ALS suggests telling them what is happening at the time. We are being honest with Sara, but there is no point in worrying her about things that she can't do anything about. It is not helpful to tell her that ALS has a life expectancy of three to five years. Besides, only God knows how long I will live.

So we are taking pictures and writing stories about fun times, building up as many memories as we can while we have time. And we are answering questions as they are being asked.

KRISTIN'S JOURNAL, APRIL 2011: *My Calling*

Between dealing with our insurance, managing Todd's health with supplements and massages, taking care of the kids, and picking up more of the household responsibilities, I have a lot on my plate these days.

On occasion, I wistfully think of how much easier my life was a year ago. I miss Todd's help with the housework. He was an amazing cleaner and this is an area where I do not excel. And I miss the perfect omelets he used to cook for me on Saturday mornings. I also miss sleeping in on weekends when Todd would get up early with the kids, but now Todd really needs his sleep or his muscles don't do well, so I get up willingly, although I am sleepy and sometimes grumpy when I get up. The thoughts about "before" are fleeting though, because for the most part, I focus on what we have. I am glad that Todd is still here with us and our marriage is strong. I am thankful for our children and the memories we have. And I am thankful that Todd is doing relatively well today.

A year ago, we had a guest speaker at church, a missionary who trains pastors in Africa and other poor, dangerous places throughout the world. He shared stories of the scary things he has faced, and then said, "There is no safer place for you than where God wants you." And I felt inspired and conflicted. Maybe I should be doing something that would make an eternal difference, in addition to raising our own children, of course. Maybe I should join the mission's committee. But I was busy with a new baby, so I didn't get around to looking into it, and then Todd was diagnosed. I don't struggle with whether or not I should be doing something else anymore. As Todd faces ALS, I have a clear sense of purpose, "to love and to cherish, until death do us part;" that is an all-consuming calling for this season of my life. And I am glad I can do it.

OUR PRAYER

God, Your Word says, "Whoever finds his life will lose it, but whoever loses his life for my sake will find it." (Matthew 10:39) As we face the losses that accompany ALS, we find meaning in losing our lives. As we face disease and experience weakness in our bodies, we experience Your strength in our souls. As caregivers, we pick up more responsibilities as we give to our loved one and find joy as we 'lose our life' in service. As we experience suffering, we lose our lives for Your sake.

2 CORINTHIANS 4:16-18 Therefore, we do not lose heart. Though outwardly we are wasting away, yet inwardly we are being renewed day by day. For our light and momentary troubles are achieving for us an eternal glory that far outweighs them all. So we fix our eyes not on what is seen, but on what is unseen. For what is seen is temporary, but what is unseen is eternal.

21.

EMBRACING LIFE

May the God of hope fill you with all
joy and peace as you trust in him,
so that you may overflow with hope
by the power of the Holy Spirit.
—*Romans 15:13*

Kristin and I try to give Sara and Isaac a warning before ending the fun, "One more minute, and then we will need to go." They run around frantically—at the park, in the pool, wherever—playing with their favorite things before playtime is up. Since my diagnosis, I have been doing the same thing with my life—trying to take it all in while I still have time.

"Guillermo," I asked my colleague who was visiting from Argentina, "do you want to go out for lunch?" He had been in our office for a week, it was Friday, and he would be staying over the weekend to attend meetings the following week. "I will see if anybody else wants to go."

I recruited Oscar, another Argentinean who had lived in the U.S. for years. I like Oscar because we share common interests. He has realized more dreams than I: He loves sailing; I love boating—he actually has a sailboat. He loves languages; I love word etymology—he actually speaks more than one language, six to be exact. He loves history; so do I—he actually knows more American history than I do. We both love photography, and we have agreed that we should go out together and take photos this summer. I have a feeling I'll learn a lot from him. He has also faced death—he is an eight-year survivor of stage-four cancer.

An interest we do not share, however, is his love for cars. I suggested that we ride with Guillermo who was given a roomy, four-door Ford Escape SUV by the rental car company. My truck was out of the question, of course, as more than two of us were going to lunch. However, Oscar insisted that we take his car. "It has two doors, right?" I asked, incredulous at his suggestion.

"It's okay. Somebody can sit in the back," he reassured me. I did not argue with him. *It may be cramped, but it would be fun to ride in his BMW convertible.*

As we approached the car, Guillermo said, "I'll sit in back."

"Oh, no. I'll be fine," I said. "You sit up front."

As Oscar backed out of the parking spot and put the car in first gear, he accelerated hard and I was pressed against the back seat. Even so, the seat was so small that I was still part of the conversation. Oscar explained how much he loved his car—a BMW 335i M-Sport convertible—and the acceleration.

"I thought BMWs were doggie at slow speeds, and only really performed at the top end," I said, not doubting that it was quick after a couple stop signs and a few corners.

"But this is a 3.0 liter with twin turbos," he explained.

"Isn't there a delay before the turbo kicks in?"

"They have two turbos, one for slow speed and one for fast speeds. There is no delay—watch." He punched it and accelerated away from another stop sign. Oscar has a zest for life, something that seems common among those who have survived a life-threatening disease.

After lunch, I asked Guillermo if he wanted to head over to my house as I needed to pick up a box of old electronics that had to be dropped off at a hazardous waste collection point. I told him that I could use help carrying the box, and it would give him a chance to see more of Racine and a typical American house.

I was not concerned about bringing Guillermo back to our house as Kristin had just whipped it into shape for a showing at 11:30 that morning. The house was in perfect shape, and Kristin had called to say that she was running late and wouldn't be home, so I would not be surprising her. Our house is typically not in a condition to have unexpected guests.

After showing Guillermo around, he asked why we were selling. At that point, many of my colleagues knew of my diagnosis, but Guillermo, being from Argentina, did not know. I explained to him that I had a neurological disease that would eventually result in my paralysis. For my international friends, I typically don't describe my disease as ALS, as it has no meaning to most people outside of the United States and Canada. I explained that I would need a handicap-accessible home all on one level that I would be able to navigate in a wheelchair. Then I said in passing, "I have a disease called ALS."

"Yes," he said, "I understand. I know ALS. My son has Duchenne disease."

"I am so sorry to hear that."

"That's life." Guillermo shrugged.

Duchenne disease is one of the most common muscular dystrophies. It's a genetic disease, only affecting males, although women can be carriers. Symptoms typically appear by age five, showing large calf and deltoid muscles. Children typically end up in braces by age ten. Life span is limited to thirty-five to forty years. In this case there is a known cause, but that is little reassurance, as the outcome is the same. And it is so much more unfair, affecting children at such a young age. Guillermo's son is thirteen. He started having symptoms when he was much younger. It is so unfair.

I had known about Duchenne disease, as it was one of the many diseases that I studied while looking for any other possible reason for my symptoms. There were several other diseases that I wished mine could be; Duchenne disease was not one of them.

Guillermo and I talked in a way that is difficult to talk with many others. He shared that he is somewhat private about his situation; he used to tell more people at work, but he realized that they felt sorry for him, and he did not want people to feel sorry for him.

"I understand," I said. "I don't want to talk about ALS all the time. There is more to my life than the disease. At first, I was reluctant to tell many people because I was not ready to accept it myself." I told those in my church and a few people at work, like my manager who needed to know why I was taking off so much time for doctors' appointments. But once I fully accepted that I had ALS, I was more open about it. As the news spread, I kept having awkward conversations: "I just heard; I am so sorry."

"Kristin and I signed up for a contest," I told Guillermo, "and there was a story written about us in the paper. Now people know, and it is kind of a relief because I don't have to explain it over and over again. And we thought that if anything good were to come of this, it would be showing others that there can be peace and joy even when someone knows that he is going to die. And I hope they see that my joy and peace comes from Christ."

"Yes, faith is important," Guillermo said, nodding, then fell silent.

That's life. Pain and suffering are as much a part of life as a fun, carefree ride in a convertible. Guillermo is not keeping his son's condition a secret; he just doesn't go around telling everybody because it's not central in his everyday life. He showed me pictures of his family—normal vacation pictures in which everyone was smiling, even his son. There is pain and suffering in this world, but there is also joy, and not just suffering *here* and joy *there*, but suffering *and* joy in the very same place.

KRISTIN'S JOURNAL, APRIL 2011:
Finding Strength

We received feedback from the showing last week. The buyer liked our house, but they put an offer on a house closer to work; our house was their second choice. At least the feedback was good. My mom said, "It's like what I said when you thought you would never find someone to marry. I kept telling you, 'It only takes one.'" So we are waiting for the right one at the right time to come along and fall in love with our house.

Todd's left arm has really atrophied. As I massaged it last night, I noticed that it is as thin as mine. The muscle loss has been gradual, but relentless. Todd is thinking about getting an arm sling-when he can rest his arm on his desk at work it is okay, but, on the weekends, it gets sore dangling there. He can pour a glass of water from a gallon jug when it is half full, but when it is full, it is too heavy for him.

In an article about living with ALS written by a neurologist, she says, "The time of receiving the diagnosis is the worst part. It changes your whole life. Once you adjust to the diagnosis and understand ALS better, it gets more manageable."[13] As we approach the first anniversary of Todd's diagnosis, I have come to accept that this is our life, that ALS is what it is, that it is progressing, that we can live with Todd's ALS and be sad and find joy at the same time.

I have thought a lot about how Todd's ALS will affect Sara and Isaac. Christina Rasmussen wrote a book called Dance with Grief. Her nine-year-old daughter asked her, "Mommy, what does it mean to dance with grief? How can you dance when you are crying?" Christina reminded her of the days they spent at the beach having fun in the waves after her daddy died. Her daughter remembered having fun while they were still sad. "I can always have the same feelings about daddy even though I am having fun." There is deep sadness in loss, but there can also be joy at the same time.[14]

Sara and Isaac have not had to grieve for our situation yet. I am glad that I got a heads-up of what the future holds so I can work through it before they have to. When it is time for them to grieve, I will be a stronger mom to help them, hold them, cry with them, and find joy in living, even then.

I continue to pray for a miraculous healing for Todd each night. At the same time, I feel God giving me strength to face this situation. I talked to another woman whose husband has ALS. She acknowledges that her faith isn't what it should be but still says, "I must be getting strength from someone."

OUR PRAYER
*God, You are getting us through
these difficult times.*

PHILIPPIANS 4:13 *I can do everything
through him who gives me strength.*

22.

MAKING LEMONADE

And we know that in all things God works
for the good of those who love him, who
have been called according to his purpose.
—*Romans 8:28*

Kristin had the large red suitcase in the middle of the living room floor. "I packed our stuff," Kristin said; "my, Sara's, and Isaac's clothes. I need you to pack your clothes and they need to fit in here. We'll check this one bag and both car seats, and then we'll have our carry-ons." She explained the plan to me a few days before our flight was to depart for California on a Saturday in mid-May 2011.

Sara walked into the room, holding her doll. "I want to bring Annika," Sara said.

"You can bring whatever you can carry in your backpack," Kristin told her.

"Now that you have to carry everything, you pack light," I said in amusement, thinking of the multiple bags I had to lug through the airport a little over a year ago on our family vacation to Florida. Then a few weeks after that trip, concerned with one weak bicep, I saw the spine-care specialist. Since then, the ALS had progressed slowly, but steadily. My right arm was as weak as my left was a year prior. Both hands had become so weak that I could only type in thirty-second spurts, so I relied on dictation software. My legs were still strong, but stiff and spastic, and they fatigued with anything more than moderate walking.

We were hesitant to go on a family vacation because we needed to save money for the down payment on the Christmas Tree House, especially if we would end up dumping our house for any less than we were asking. But memories are important, and God provided with generous gifts from a couple of our friends.

We planned to spend two nights in Los Angeles, staying with friends. We would then drive to San Diego to stay at a condominium that somebody graciously provided for free, and then drive back to Anaheim and spend a day at Disneyland.

"I sent an e-mail to Joni and Friends. Maybe we can visit their ministry while we're there," Kristin told me. "Joni and Friends has done so much to help disabled people across the world. It would be really cool to see it."

In California we visited our old friends, Grant and Chantel. They relocated to Los Angeles with their triplets, who are a year younger than Sara, and their fourth child, who is Isaac's age. They rent a house in Bel Air on top of a foothill of the Santa Monica Mountains, with a beautiful view of downtown L.A. twelve miles in the distance. The backyard is fifteen feet deep, a manicured lawn bordered by a flower garden and a fence separating the yard from the steep slope to the ravine below. Grant and I stood in the backyard looking at a lemon tree next to the fence.

"I think they grafted a winter tree and a summer tree together, because it gives fruit all year long," Grant explained. There were a few large, yellow lemons on the lawn side of the tree and a dozen more dangling over the ravine.

Grant and I became friends in Milwaukee years ago. He had just graduated from the Chicago School of Business, but he was originally a Minnesota boy, like I was. We found a connection in our background, golf, and Christ. He and I met at church, where I also met Kristin. Grant attended my wedding a few months after I met him, and then, I stood up in his wedding two years later. We haven't always stayed in touch, but whenever we reconnect we can pick up from where we left off. Grant has a special place in my heart because I became friends with him during the time that my heart was softening.

Prior to moving to Milwaukee, my heart was cold and broken. I tried to live life my way and I saw the impact that sin had on my life and on the lives of others. I was healthy and successful, but I didn't have joy. I knew I needed a change so I looked for work out-of-state. I landed in Milwaukee, and then connected with a good church. God used people in that church to soften my heart. It started with a lady—I never asked her name—who greeted me every Sunday so warmly and made me feel welcomed. It continued with friendships I formed with men of God, including Grant. And, the best of all, I fell in love with Kristin, who is a gracious and godly woman. I recommitted my life to Christ, not just believing He is the Son of God and that He died for my sins, which I have known in my head since I was a boy, but trusting and following Him in my day-to-day life.

Though it didn't happen overnight, my heart softened, and I came to have real joy in life. I still struggle with a host of shortcomings. I'm not always content. At times, I'm impertinent. But I know that if I seek Him, I can find more joy and peace than anything the world has to offer. God loves me and He wants the best for me. "God is love. Whoever lives in love lives in God, and God in him" (1 John 4:16b). Because of this love—God loving me, and me now being able to love others—before I leave for work, I kiss Isaac, Sara, and Kristin, three times each on their foreheads and tell them, "God loves you; I love you; have a good day."

After Grant pointed out a few sights in the distance, I asked if I could pick lemons to make lemonade.

"Go for it."

I picked a few within reach on the lawn-side. Grant retrieved his hockey stick to pull the prime lemons that were hanging over the ravine close enough to pick.

I made a basket out of the front of my T-shirt, put the lemons in it, and went to find Sara in the house. "Sara, do you want to make lemonade?"

"Yea!" she exclaimed, wanting entertainment while the triplets napped.

Chantel set us up with an electric lemon squeezer.

"I know how to make lemonade," Sara said.

"How did you learn to make lemonade?"

"From Elmo! The first thing you need to make lemonade is lemons. We need three lemons, four cups of water, and one scoop of sugar," she said, referring to Elmo and Grover's Lemonade Stand, a Sesame Street game she plays on the Internet.

I cut the lemons in half and placed each half in the grinder. Sara helped me press down on the lemons; she wanted to help because it was fun, but I really needed her assistance.

"Sara," I said, "when life gives you lemons, make lemonade."

"What does that mean?"

"It means that we need to make the best of what we are given. Lemons are not much use on their own. They're too sour. But we can use them to make something else that is good. That's what God does with our lives; whatever happens, He uses it for good."

I have the joy and peace that comes with knowing Christ, but knowing Christ does not mean that I'm free from all the trouble in the world. All blessings come from God, but God doesn't promise them. Can He heal? Yes, but everybody in the history of this earth, except for Enoch and Elijah, eventually faced death. God does not promise health and prosperity, but He does say that He'll work for good in all things for those who love Him.

Living well is really about making lemonade out of my situation. God wants us to have a certain response to adversity. Is that to be stoic and pretend like one is not affected? No. In the biblical story of Job facing suffering, "Job got up and tore his robe and shaved his head. Then he fell to the ground in worship. He was stricken with grief, and then he said, 'Naked I came from my mother's womb, and naked I will depart. The LORD gave and the LORD has taken away; may the name of the LORD be praised.' In all this, Job did not sin by charging God with wrongdoing" (Job 1:20–22). God is sovereign; He allowed me to be stricken with ALS. He gave me this life; it is not mine to keep, and if He decides to take this life from me sooner than I had planned, then I mustn't hold on to it too tightly. I don't need to like it, but I must continue to praise God and do His will.

God wants us to be content with our own limitations so that we trust in Christ more. Christ says, "My grace is sufficient for you, for my power is made perfect in weakness." Paul then says, "Therefore I will boast all the more gladly about my weaknesses, so that Christ's power may rest on me. That is why, for Christ's sake, I delight in weaknesses, in insults, in hardships, in persecutions, in difficulties. For when I am weak, then I am strong" (2 Corinthians 12:9–10). I've heard people say that Christianity is a crutch; I say that Christ is more than my crutch. He is my walker, my wheelchair.

I pray nightly the same prayer, "God, I pray for miraculous healing, but if that is not Your will, I pray for slow progression.

At least, God, give me joy and peace." Though I pray for healing, I know that it may not be God's will. I sometimes think that prayer is not just a way for us to ask God for what we want; rather, it is a way for God to help us understand what He wants. In Christ's prayer in Gethsemane, He prayed that the cup would be taken from Him, but then He prayed "Your will be done." Above all else, I need to ask that God's will be done.

So what is God's will? I believe it is to glorify Him—to recognize Him for who He is, to give Him the credit for all that's good in the world, and to choose a godly response to adversity. Having ALS gives me the great opportunity to glorify God. How easy it was for me to be happy when I had good health, a good job, a beautiful wife and two wonderful kids. But with a terminal disease, I can speak with authority—God is good, He is working for good in this situation, and I am choosing to make the best of it; I am making lemonade.

Before heading south to San Diego, we drove north to Agoura Hills to see the Joni and Friends ministry. We pulled up to a large office building with dozens of cars, and then went inside where our tour guide greeted us.

"Is this whole building Joni and Friends?" Kristin asked.

"Yes."

"How many employees do you have?"

"About seventy."

We were given a tour of the building. The guide explained the many ways in which the ministry served the disabled with family camps, literary resources, and a radio ministry. Two hundred fifty dollars could purchase a wheelchair, made in a California prison, that would be given to a disabled person somewhere in the world. We looked at beautiful paintings decorating the walls; Joni had painted them using only her mouth.

Joni believes that a disabled life is a life worth living. She has made lemonade out of lemons, and the cool thing about lemonade is that it is really good. The disabled life can be a really good life, maybe even better than the life that would have been, especially when it is filled with Christ's love.

Joni wanted to meet us. She had just finished taping her radio show, and we waited while a photographer took her picture. The kids were restless, but our guide graciously entertained Sara with a book while Isaac ran around.

Joni came out and greeted us. She asked, "So what's your story?"

I told her about the diagnosis and the major events over the previous year. "I am so much more focused now on what's important in life," I said. "Life is fuller and has more meaning. I'm not sure I would've ever gotten to this place if I had stayed healthy. It is quite liberating in a way."

"Yes, it is liberating," she agreed.

"But I think I would still rather be healthy and not have grown so much." I laughed.

Before we left, I asked to take a picture with her.

"I made a decision last year to splurge on this camera. Photography is my art," I told her, realizing I was far from the artist that she was, but knowing that she would understand.

We followed her into her office. Joni used her mouth to sign a children's book and she gave it to Sara. I set up the big Canon 5D camera and instructed our guide on how to focus and snap the picture. I stood behind Joni, with a large smile, inspired by her and imagining a life of meaning and hope. Joni chose a godly response to adversity in her life, and I will too.

KRISTIN'S JOURNAL, APRIL 2011:
Keep Living

Sometimes, I feel stuck as I continue to process what we are going through. I read books written by people who have suffered—spiritual giants who encourage me and minister to so many. They seem to have wrapped their minds around why God has allowed suffering in their lives and in the world. I feel more like Job when he was questioning God: "Your hands shaped me and made me. Will you now turn and destroy me?" (Job 10:8)

"I feel like I am failing God's Sovereignty 101," I told Jana. "All these people have it all figured out."

"I am sure they didn't have it figured out at the beginning of their journey," she said. Jana reminds me that I don't need to have it all together or have all the answers. It takes time to mourn our losses.

"I'm so sad," I told my counselor last fall.

"It is sad," he agreed. "When you read stories, they have happy parts and sad parts. This is a sad part of your story."

As our journey continues, I know that there will be difficult times in front of us, and I am not done grieving. I know there will be more pain. I may not be done with anger or depression, but I no longer feel like my life is over. I am learning to keep living while grieving.

OUR PRAYER

God, we may not be able to grasp Your sovereignty or know Your purpose in our suffering, but we do know You are with us, giving us strength. We know You love us and our children. We know You are good. We thank You for Your presence in our lives.

ISAIAH 40:28-31 *Do you not know? Have you not heard? The Lord is the everlasting God, the Creator of the ends of the earth. He will not grow tired or weary, and his understanding no one can fathom. He gives strength to the weary and increases the power of the weak. Even youths grow tired and weary, and young men stumble and fall; but those who hope in the Lord will renew their strength. They will soar on wings like eagles; they will run and not grow weary, they will walk and not be faint.*

23.

LIVING A LIFE OF MEANING

Praise be to the God and Father of our Lord Jesus Christ, the Father of compassion and the God of comfort, who comforts us in all our troubles, so that we can comfort those in any trouble with the comfort we ourselves have received from God.
—2 Corinthians 1:3–4

In early June 2011, nearly one year after my diagnosis, it was a little past 9:00 p.m. on a Friday and I had tucked Sara into bed, read her a book, said our prayers together, and sung her a song. The song was one that Kristin wrote, sung to the tune of *Brahms' Lullaby*:

Lullaby and good night,
Go to sleep my sweet Sara.
Close your eyes and let the fairies
Come and sprinkle their fairy dust.
You'll fly through the sky,
And you'll soar like a bird.
You'll slide down the rainbow,
What a beautiful world.

I went downstairs; Kristin was still upstairs putting Isaac to bed—typically a forty-minute process that involves her lying next to his crib and patting his back whenever he protests. I sat at our six-year-old Compaq computer and cleaned up the hard drive, which was nearly full. I started with 1.7 GB of free space and, after twenty minutes, I was up to 10.8. I made sure all our files were backed up to an external drive so I could transfer them to the new computer scheduled to arrive the following week. I was getting that Apple MacBook Pro, the computer I will use to edit videos for the kids.

The phone rang.

I answered it. "Hello?"

"Hi. You don't know me…," a timid voice began, and then trailed off, so soft I could barely tell if it was a man or a woman. "Are you Todd?"

"Yes, this is Todd. What is your name?" I asked gently.

"My name is Violet. When I saw your picture, I cried."

"Where did you see my picture?"

"In the paper. My son is in the same situation as you. He was diagnosed with ALS two years ago. I cried for two days after I saw your picture. You look a lot like my son."

"Tell me more about him." I leaned forward and placed my left elbow on the desk to better support the phone.

"He doesn't work anymore, but before he left, his company threw him a big benefit."

"Is your son Eric?" I knew of one other person in the area with ALS and the story sounded familiar.

"Yes. How did you know?" she asked, her voice more sure.

"His sister Susan drew my blood a year ago after I was first diagnosed. She told me about Eric." I had over a half dozen vials of blood drawn for various tests that my general practitioner wanted to run. Susan was amazed at the number of draws I needed, and she could see the sadness on my face. I shared with her that I might have ALS, but was looking for another cause. She told me about her brother.

"Susan's good at drawing blood, isn't she?" Violet asked proudly.

"Yes. She's the best there is. We talked for a while, and she gave me Eric's number. I never did call him."

"You should call him," Violet said. "He would like that."

"Yes, but it is hard for me to think of the future. How is he doing?"

"He's in a wheelchair. It's hard for him to get around. All of the family functions are at his house. But I haven't seen him for a while, because I have a hard time getting down my stairs," she said, a hint of sadness in her voice. "I am eighty-one."

Violet told me the names and ages of her other kids, and then told me more about Eric. He was her youngest and had just turned forty-two. "But that can't be right. I was thirty-nine when I had him. He was born in May, and then I turned forty shortly after that."

"Well, the math works. Happy Birthday. You are turning eighty-two."

"Oh, I suppose I am," she said, delightfully surprised.

"Eric and I have that in common. I'm the youngest of the family too, and we both were diagnosed at about the same age," I said. "My mother is going through the same thing that you are. It's hard to see your baby suffer, isn't it?"

"That's what I call him—my baby. Do you hate being called the baby?"

"No," I said. "I wear it like a badge of honor."

She laughed. "I like you. You remind me a lot of Eric. Did you ever play baseball?"

"No."

"I wonder if that might have been how he got it," Violet said.

"I do not know. I doubt it. They haven't found a cause. I used to spend a lot of time wondering what might have triggered my ALS. I eventually came to realize that knowing how it started will bring me no closer to curing it. This is what happens in life: We are born, we live, and then we die. There are many ways to die—but it is not about how we die; rather, life is about how we live. And our purpose while we live, whether we have forty years or eighty years, is to glorify God."

Violet told me she hoped Eric gets a ventilator. Kristin and I have discussed this option on occasion, but I haven't yet decided what I will do.

"That is a personal decision. It is a hard decision, and there is no right answer. Some decide not to get a ventilator, and that is okay. The Lord gives and the Lord takes away. This is not our life. It belongs to God. If God allows our bodies to fail sooner in life, then it is okay that we not hold on to it too tightly. It is the natural course of this disease. Others choose to get a ventilator, and that is great, as life can have meaning and joy, even with no mobility."

"He is being positive for his family," Violet said. "I wish I could see him. It's so hard for me to get out of my house. And I worry too much. They didn't even tell me that he was sick for the first year because they knew I would worry. Well, I'm his mom, and that's what I do, and that's not going to change."

"I am sure Eric would love to see you, and that he would not expect you to be strong for him. If he is like me, then he has come to see this as a blessing, in a way, because this disease gives us time to grieve with our family. There are a lot of ways to die, and none of them are good. But, with this disease, we will have a few years, maybe ten, to say a long Minnesota goodbye, as I would say back home."

"It was so good to talk to you," Violet said. "I should let you go. Your ear must be getting tired."

"Yes, I should go. But it's not my ear that's getting tired. It's my arm that's getting tired trying to hold up this phone."

"You're funny." She chuckled.

"Call me anytime that you want to talk."

When we agreed to an interview for the local paper, I told Kristin that it would be a good thing if we could bless even one person in the process. One needn't do anything spectacular or grand. Living a life of meaning can be as simple as a conversation with an eighty-one-year-old mother. Or it can be as simple as being a continued presence in the life of my family, and eventually, when I am unable to talk, they will see in my eyes how proud I am of them.

On Saturday morning, the temperature was eighty degrees and the sun was shining bright at 9:00 a.m. when five students and a college staff member arrived to do yard work and plant flowers for us. The students were from Shepherd's College, a three-year post-secondary educational program for individuals with intellectual disabilities. They attend our church, and, after hearing our story, asked if they could volunteer their services to help us on the weekend before their graduation. Two of the students were horticulture majors, so they offered to lead the planting project at our house.

Kristin showed the three women—Julie, Lisa and Megan—and the staff member where she wanted flowers planted along the front and side of the house. I gave the two men—Tim and Daniel—shovels and a wheelbarrow to dig up a strip of lawn behind the house to prepare it for new sod.

The men went to work on the three-by-twenty-foot strip mostly covered in clover. Tim began sweating as he tossed scoop after scoop of dirt into the wheelbarrow.

Kristin pulled Isaac in the red wagon to the back patio to watch the action. Sara helped with her green plastic shovel, looking for worms. "Here's one," Tim said, dangling it in front of her.

"I'll put it in my worm farm," Sara said, then opened the lid of the old salad container full of dirt that she keeps in the backyard. "Now, I have six."

Daniel paced his work while he tried to engage Tim in conversation. Tim, who was being careful to avoid a clay drainage pipe that stuck up in the middle of the lawn, said, "Don't talk to me right now, Daniel. I'm thinking really hard about not hitting that drain." After he removed the dirt from around the drain, Tim told Kristin, "I do a lot of work like this. My internship is on a farm."

"That's why I keep asking him what I should do today," Daniel said. "I'm a culinary arts major."

Julie came to the back patio and asked for a shovel. "Can you give me a high five?" she asked Isaac, who sat strapped in the wagon. The guys had the digging under control, so I followed Julie to check on the women's work.

The women were inspecting the flowers they had planted on the side of the house. "Do you think these flowers are too close?" Lisa asked Megan.

"Let's ask Tim."

"Come look at these flowers, Tim," Lisa yelled.

Tim came around the house and examined the flowers. "Those two are too close." As Tim and I started to walk to the back patio, he asked me, "How are you feeling?"

"Weak," I said, "but there's no pain."

I am honest when people ask. They want to know; that is why they ask. There is no sugar-coating ALS, but I show them with my smile that I am okay.

"I'm so sad for you." Tim stopped and studied my face.

"Thanks. We all have things we need to deal with," I said.

The students finished the work within a couple hours. We

were blessed by their help, and they enjoyed helping us. We thanked them as they climbed back into the van. "Congratulations on your graduation," Kristin told them.

The students were excited for the next weekend. Some of them had jobs lined up; others were still waiting to see what God had in store for them. They would be graduating one year from the day of my diagnosis—June 11.

A year ago, I did not see any hope, and I wondered what purpose I would have in life with a disability. Now I see purpose and meaning in my life and in the lives of others who suffer from their own challenges. Suffering is part of the human condition, and even Christ calls us to share in His suffering. Perhaps in doing so, our hearts are opened to love and to be loved with a love that comes closer to God's love.

KRISTIN'S JOURNAL, JUNE 2011:
Join in Suffering

Every time I look at my new flowers, I smile, inspired by the college students who planted them for us. My perspective on suffering has changed this past year. I used to feel bad for those who had a disability. Now, I find inspiration from the many people who are living meaningful lives in spite of, and sometimes because of, big challenges. If they can face their difficult circumstances, and continue to follow God and live well, I want to do the same in my situation. We all have something to give.

In the past, I often didn't know what to say to people who were suffering. Now that my husband has ALS and I have experienced a year of intense grief, I am more empathetic. Even with the benefits of spiritual growth, if I had a choice, I would not have signed up for this journey, but that is not up to me. All I can choose is my response.

But there is a man who signed up to join us in suffering. Jesus lived a full purposeful life, knowing he was going to die a cruel, painful death. Then He went to the cross and suffered as He died for our sin. In Philippians 3, Paul writes, "I consider everything a loss compared to the surpassing greatness of knowing Christ...I want to know Christ and the power of his resurrection and the fellowship of sharing in his sufferings, becoming like him in his death." In the past year, I have tried to understand how to approach suffering by reading scripture and other books written by people who have lived with suffering for years. At times, I've thought I've figured some of it out, but then it doesn't stick and I slip back into worry and fear and I need to relearn things. When I continue reading Philippians 3, I am encouraged because Paul writes that he hasn't arrived either, "not that I have already obtained all this, or have already been made perfect, but I press on to take hold of that for which Christ Jesus took hold of me." So I, too, keep on going. God got us through this past year. He will be with us in our uncertain future.

OUR PRAYER

God, we look to Jesus and the cross in our suffering and we pray that we will know You and Your love more deeply. And as we face challenges, we pray You will use our pain for Your glory.

MATTHEW 11:28 *Jesus said, "Come to me, all of you who are weary and carry heavy burdens, and I will give you rest." (NLT)*

NOTES

1. *Shadowlands*, Dir. Richard Attenborough. Perf. Anthony Hopkins, Debra Winger. Videocassette. Savoy Pictures, 1993.
2. Catherine Lomen-Hoerth, interview in *Your Resource Guide to Living a Fuller Life with ALS* (ALS Association, n.d.), 15. Accessed April 29, 2013, from http://www.alsa.org/assets/pdfs/brochures/living_fuller_life.pdf.
3. In the months after Todd's diagnosis, we found comfort in JJ Heller's music, especially the song "Your Hands," *Painted Red* (Stone Table Records, 2008).
4. When courting, we found David Keirsey's expansion of Myers-Briggs' work invaluable in understanding each other's character and temperament types as described in *Please Understand Me II* (Del Mar: Prometheus Nemesis Book Company, 1998.)
5. We enjoyed sitting under the teaching of Pastor Marc Erickson at Eastbrook Church in Milwaukee, Wisconsin.
6. We are still learning the lessons discussed in Larry Crabb's book *Shattered Dreams: God's Unexpected Pathway to Joy* (Colorado Springs: WaterBrook Press, 2001). We appreciate his treatment of the story of Ruth and Naomi.
7. Jack Nicholson and Morgan Freeman play two terminally ill men who embark on a road trip to complete a wish-list of things to do before they die in *The Bucket List*, Dir. Rob Reiner. Warner Bros., 2007.

8. http://www.LifewithALS.com

9. We gleaned this insight from a sermon by Pastor David Sincock of Fellowship Baptist Church in Racine, Wisconsin.

10. Christina Rasmussen's website *Second Firsts* at http://www.secondfirsts.com/.

11. We are thankful for the ministry of Joni Eareckson Tada. After Todd's diagnosis, we found comfort and insight in Joni's books, especially *A Lifetime of Wisdom: Embracing the Way God Heals You* (Grand Rapids: Zondervan, 2009) and *A Place of Healing: Wrestling with the Mysteries of Suffering, Pain, and God's Sovereignty* (Colorado Springs: David C. Cook, 2010). Joni says that she gets out of bed in the morning, goes through an elaborate routine to get ready for the day, and endures pain on her commute to Joni and Friends Center for the sake of her purpose: to go out, find the disabled and bring them in. *A Place of Healing*, 110.

12. Joni describes an incident in which someone accused her of not having enough faith to be healed in *A Place of Healing*, 15–17.

13. Catherine Lomen-Hoerth, interview in *Your Resource Guide to Living a Fuller Life with ALS* (ALS Association, n.d.), 15. Accessed April 29, 2013, from http://www.alsa.org/assets/pdfs/brochures/living_fuller_life.pdf.

14. Christina Rasmussen, April 29, 2011, "Dance With Grief." Accessed April 29, 2013, from http://www.secondfirsts.com/2011/04/dance-with-grief/.

In 2012, we sold our house in Racine and moved to Michigan where we built a handicap-accessible house next to Kristin's parents. Thank you to the many people who gave of their time, skills, and finances to help us build The Christmas Tree House.

Visit www.NevaStory.com to journey with us.

Thank you to the many friends and professionals who helped edit and bring structure to *Heavy*.

Made in the USA
Charleston, SC
05 July 2014